LEAN
LEADERSHIP

MARTA FERREIRA

LEAN LEADERSHIP

From Manager to Leader

MONTEREY
PRESS

First Published in 2012
by Monterey Press
PO Box 319
Carlton North VIC 3054
Australia
www.montereypress.com

Author contact: info@aleanbook.com
Website: www.aleanbook.com

Cover design by Pedro Farelo
Designed and typeset by Sue Balcer of JustYourType.biz

National Library of Australia Cataloguing-in-Publication entry:

Ferreira, Marta

Lean leadership / by Marta Ferreira

9780987056139 (pbk.)

Leadership
Organizational change--Management
Personnel management
Employee motivation

658.406

For my new family: Everton and Lucas

Projetos e sonhos como este só
são possíveis com o apoio,
amizade e companheirismo
que tenho em casa.
Obrigada pela paciência.

Acknowledgements

I would like to acknowledge the support of a number of people who contributed to making this book a reality.

Steve Gallagher is a wonderful friend and skilled practitioner who provided valuable input and guidance regarding the content of this book, ensuring it adds value to the many other books published in this topic area.

Seamus Power shared advice and first-hand, detailed explanations of how Hoshin Kanri works and is implemented in practice. Seamus is someone I look to as a mentor and is also one of very few managing directors known for their lean leadership style and their sustainable approach to implementing change in a global organization in Australia.

Huong Dang and Elizabeth Watson also offered valuable feedback and suggestions.

David Brewster's amazing patience and creativity helped me translate my sometimes complex ideas into much simpler and more accessible language. Editor Heather Kelly added the final coat of polish.

I would also like to thank my husband, Everton Böing, for sharing his knowledge of sustainability and for his input into parts of the story to ensure the reader would understand that, for example, change only happens – unfortunately – when it's forced.

And to my family and friends for their strength and ongoing belief that I should tell my story – thank you.

Contents

Preface

Hundreds — no, thousands — of books have been published on leadership, so you could be forgiven for picking up this book and asking why there needs to be another. The reason is quite simple. In the work I have done as a manager and consultant over more than a dozen years, I still see the same weaknesses in leadership over and over again. I still see the same situations over and over again: leaders and their people struggling to understand their goals, let alone achieve them. And I still see the same potential over and over again: the potential for leaders and their people to work together much more effectively, if only they had some simple management techniques and tools available to them. So there is still plenty of scope for leadership lessons to be taught.

Lean Leadership tells the story of Charlie, a middle manager in a chocolate factory, and his team. With the company under threat from widening global competition, there is an urgent need for change. In the past Charlie, as the leader, has always seen it as his role to drive change. Now, as Charlie struggles with his own personal challenges, he needs to do things differently. Now he needs to start sharing the responsibility for change with his team leaders and the rest of his staff. Charlie and his team learn that when they work together to identify and implement improvements to the way they work, the job is easier for everyone – and the results surpass anything they thought possible. Along the way they discover a number of simple but remarkably powerful tools to help them on their journey. These tools, and the way in which Charlie and his team use them, can be implemented by any leader in any organization.

The concepts behind *Lean Leadership*, including the tools described here, have a long heritage. Many of them have been 'best practice' in many industries – especially manufacturing – for over fifty years. But in the way they are presented here, they have much broader application. Whether you work in a bank, an insurance company, a retail chain, a hospital or almost anywhere else, you and your team can benefit from the lessons learnt over a long time by these companies. They include focusing on what is important, involving and empowering the whole team to get things done, sharing information openly, and constantly learning from past experiences.

Of course, the scenarios presented in a story like this should always be seen as general examples. While Charlie and his team are faced with specific goals, and while they go about using the tools to meet those goals in a specific way, what is important to you, the reader, are the general principles and logic behind what they do. For instance, while the factory's goal here is to cut costs by 20 per cent over a year, that goal could easily have been to increase productivity by a similar amount, or to grow sales or market share, or any of myriad other targets. What is important is not the main goal, but the fact that the goals developed by Charlie's team make contributions that are clearly aligned with that main goal.

Some readers may already be familiar with some of the terminology used in this book — things like the 'PDCA' cycle. I would urge you to put aside any preconceptions you have about this terminology and to concentrate on the way the tools have been applied here. Many of the tools demonstrated in this book have a reputation for being made overly complicated or for having relevance only in specific situations (e.g. projects), but the reality is that when they are used properly, they can be very simple to both understand and use.

If, having read this story, you want to learn more about the concepts presented here, you will find further information and suggested reading at the end of the book. In addition, tools you can use in your own work are available by registering at *www.aleanbook.com*. Enter the promotional code L2E0A1D2, when prompted after registration, for access to additional, reader-only materials.

1   Challenge

The doctor placed the clipboard back on the end of the bed and looked down at Charlie with a steady gaze.

"You're a lucky man, Charlie. A lot of people who have heart attacks in your condition don't make it. This was only a fairly minor arrest, but you need to take it as a serious warning sign. If you have another attack it will probably not be so kind to you."

Charlie gave an expressionless nod then turned his head and stared blankly out the window. The doctor waited, allowing a good amount of time for what he'd just said to sink in.

"If you're going to get out of this dangerous situation, you're going to have to make some changes. You're going to have to change the way you eat, get more exercise and lose some weight – at least 20 kilograms for a start. And you're going to have to find a way to reduce your stress level. If you can't do those things … well, there's not much I can do to help you. Things will just continue to get worse.

"Of course I've said all that before and we've got no-where," the doctor continued. "If anything positive is going to come out of this heart attack it will be the realization that 'no change' is not an option and that this time you'll really act. But I'm also going to be more prescriptive as I'm still not sure that you can save yourself."

"Okay, Doc." Charlie fell into thought again for a moment. "So how's this going to work?"

"I'm going to write you a prescription. It won't be a prescription for medicine – it will be a prescription for lifestyle. It will be a plan to get you healthy, including an exercise regime and a diet. You'll then go away and implement that plan. Every month, you'll come and see me and we'll check on your progress. If adjustments need to be made to the plan we'll make them, but otherwise we'll just keep to the plan. We'll continue this cycle for at least 12 months: my *planning*, your *doing*, then *checking* and *adjusting* together before starting the next cycle."

More silence, then Charlie said, "The food and exercise — I reckon I can do those, even though they'll take a while and even though I've failed in the past. The sort of rigorous cycle you're talking about — I think it could work. But you also mentioned stress, and that's a different story. Problem is, I'm not really in control of that. I can't afford to leave my job, and it's my job that piles on the pressure."

"What do you do?" asked the doctor.

"I'm the operations manager in a chocolate factory," said Charlie.

"Hmm. Charlie and his very own ..." The doctor smiled. "Sorry, I'm sure you must get jokes about that all the time."

"I do," said Charlie. "But let me tell you, real life doesn't bear much resemblance to the book, let alone the movie. My job is one of long hours and constant fire fighting; one problem after the other. Half my time is spent dealing with disputes between departments, and the rest of the time I'm trying to find ways to cut costs so we can fend off competition from imports. I get to the end of each week and I'm shattered."

"But you're the Operations Manager? Aren't you in a position to do something about all those things? To identify and fix the underlying causes of the problems? Sorry, I know it sounds like a doctor's perspective — using symptoms to diagnose and fix problems is what I do all the time — but I find those fundamentals are pretty much the same in most areas of life."

"That's true, and you're right — it's my situation to fix. But I'm so snowed under most of the time that I never seem to be able to think about how we might do things better." Charlie looked down at the floor. "Then again, I guess it's just like my own situation isn't it: if nothing changes, nothing changes."

"You're right there," said the doctor. "But big changes can happen. A few years ago we streamlined our practice, taking out a whole lot of unnecessary effort. Our main goal was to be more efficient and reduce waiting-room times, but what we noticed was how much it also reduced the stress levels in the place. And it took our administration costs down substantially too — by about 30 per cent. I know we're in different situations, but my point is to encourage you to look at your challenges positively. I can't prescribe stress reduction to you, but we can certainly talk about it every time you have a check-up. I can ask you what you've done to improve the situation, just to keep you on your toes."

"Alright, Doc. Thanks. Where there's life, there's hope, I

guess." Suddenly that expression had taken on a whole new meaning.

"One other thing before you go, Charlie. I can't help thinking that working in a chocolate factory isn't the best place to be when you're trying to lose weight."

Charlie managed a smile. "Yes, perhaps a soup factory or something like that would be better. But I think I can manage to keep my hands off the product. Either that or wear a muzzle."

* * *

Charlie was released from hospital the next day.

"So what are you going to do?" asked Anna when they got home. "What are we going to do? I don't want to lose you, and the kids don't want to be without a father, so your health has to be number one. If your job is causing the stress, then quit. We'll find a way to get by. I just wish you'd acted on the doctor's advice earlier."

"I know, I know. It's my fault that it came to this. I'm the one who allowed myself to get so unfit and overweight. But there's no point dwelling on how I got to where I am. We have to be thankful that I survived, and we have to look forward. I don't think quitting work will help. As bad as it gets, it does give me purpose – something to do. I mean, what am I going to do sitting around the house all day? I won't lose 20 kilograms that way, and it would stress me out as much as work does."

"Alright," said Anna. "But promise me you'll act this time. You've been setting vague resolutions about losing weight for years and nothing has ever happened. This time something needs to change."

Charlie gave Anna a wry smile. "Your point is made. And don't worry, the doctor is on to me too. He has a plan."

Charlie went on to explain what the doctor had said to him and how they planned to work together over the next year. "He's going to write me a prescription for lifestyle: a plan to get healthy. I'll put that plan in place, with your help, then go back and see him once a month for a check-up. As we go along he'll adjust the plan if necessary, to make sure I keep making progress."

"Hmm, that's interesting," said Anna. "It sounds a lot like something we use at work. They call it 'PDCA', for 'Plan – Do – Check – Adjust'. Our general manager is always on about it – I think it must be his engineering background – but he hates us making change of any significance without using this system. He's always saying: 'If you don't plan,

how do you know what to do. If you don't check your progress, how do you know if your action was worthwhile. And if
you're not getting the results you wanted, why would you not
adjust your actions and see if you can change?' I've heard all
this so often it's ingrained in my mind, as you can tell."

At that moment the phone rang. Anna answered it
then passed the handset across to Charlie.

"It's Peter," she said. "I'll make some tea."

* * *

"How's the boss?" asked Anna after Charlie ended his call.
"Missing you?"

"He is, as a matter of fact," said Charlie. "He's not sure
how he's going to get through two weeks without me. He
didn't want to have to tell me this at the moment but the
pressure's really on. Antonio – he's the MD if you remember
– has just been to see him and the directors want a 20 per
cent reduction in costs this year. Twenty per cent! He wants
to see a plan for how we're going to do that by the end of
the month – that's only four weeks away, and I'm stuck at
home for two of those."

Charlie slumped slightly in his chair and suddenly

looked pale. Anna came and sat beside him.

"Things have to change," she said. "You simply can't take on all of this yourself. I know how much you love your chocolate factory — how many hours you put into your job, and into your people. But the fact that it is operating today, and will be again tomorrow and the day after that, shows that you have some good people there — some very capable people who I happen to know adore their boss and will do whatever they need to do to help you. I actually think you don't ask enough of your team leaders. You take on too much of the responsibility yourself. Now is the time to share the load — to get everyone to contribute to finding those cost reductions."

"But they're flat out too," said Charlie. "It's not as though they're sitting around waiting for something to do. That's part of the problem — I end up working hard to fill the holes they simply can't fill in their non-stop problem-solving days."

"Well it's like your health, Mr Barker. Unless you start doing things differently, nothing is going to change." Anna's eyes brightened. "Which gives me an idea ..." She got up and retrieved a notepad from the kitchen bench.

"You know how I mentioned that your doctor's plan sounded a lot like what we do at my work: that Plan — Do —

Check – Adjust thing. Well, I think you could use a similar approach at the factory."

Anna went on to explain that her boss used PDCA as part of a company-wide technique for implementing their strategies. "It has a fancy Japanese name, which I'm not sure I remember – Hoshin something. 'Hoshin Kanri', that's it. We just call it 'Strategy Deployment'. The Japanese phrase translates to a combination of 'compass' and 'control'. The overall concept is about providing everyone in the organization with clear direction. And once we have that direction, it's about closely monitoring our progress and making any corrections as we go along. The most important aspect of the approach is this: that the company's overall goals are directly reflected in the goals of everyone in the organization. In other words, that the strategies of the business are deployed right through the organization."

"Isn't that just common sense?" said Charlie.

"You might think so," said Anna. "But is it the way things are done at your factory now?"

Charlie shifted in his seat. "Well … no, I guess not."

"That's the thing about 'common sense'," said Anna. "Even when something makes sense, it's rarely common. How many people do you know who work at my level – two or three levels down the hierarchy – who really understand the link between the work they do and the organization's goals? In truth it hardly ever happens, which means that most people in most businesses really have no idea how what they do, individually, contributes to the whole."

Charlie thought about how frustrated he often got at the way his staff seemed to live in their own world, rarely understanding the implications of their actions beyond their own area. "I see what you mean," he said.

"The thing about all this is that it could really help you share the load amongst your team leaders," said Anna.

"I'm not sure sharing the load is going to be that easy, based on past performance," said Charlie, "but you've got me interested, so tell me more. You work in human resources, for the HR manager. Tell me how it affects your department."

"Okay. My manager, Penny – the HR manager – has a yearly plan, which is part of a longer-term five-year plan. Nothing unusual there. What's different, at least from what I've always seen in the past, is that Penny designed her plan with our help. As a group we could set whatever 'local' goals we wanted ... as long as they contributed to the company's overall goals."

"So, if you needed to cut 20 per cent of your costs

across the business, for argument's sake, Penny would be asked to make a contribution in her department. *How* she did that would be up to her and her team, including you. But *what* she did – reducing costs – was determined by that company goal."

"That's right," said Anna. "It doesn't have to be just cost cutting that is the focus. It could be revenue improvement or productivity or anything else. And it doesn't necessarily need to be an equal contribution from each department, as that would often be counterproductive. The point is that whatever plan the company comes up with, the 'mini-plans' in each department have to be in line with that plan and, as a whole, meet the plan's goals. Most importantly from your point of view, responsibility for developing and implementing those 'mini-plans' is delegated to the responsible line managers or team leaders."

"Hmm. I'm not sure. I've talked about company goals with the team in the past, but we've never really made them responsible for their direct contribution to those goals. I don't know if they'd be up to it."

Charlie thought for a while before speaking again. "Anyway, go on. What about the PDCA thing? How does that fit into this?"

Anna explained that 'Plan – Do – Check – Adjust' was the technique used to keep all these various plans on track: the overall company plan as well as each individual department's plans. "By regularly reviewing what we're doing, and using the same approach every time, it seems to keep the whole thing ticking along. And it keeps us 'in the loop'. When Penny gets us together to review our plan and some sort of change is needed – an adjustment – we all know why that's the case. There's a lot less of that typical division between managers and staff, and there are fewer misunderstandings about why decisions are being made."

Charlie was starting to be inspired by all this. It certainly made a lot of sense, though it would be a big change for his team.

"Perhaps we can talk about this some more," said Charlie. "After all, I have two weeks to sit around doing nothing before I can go back to work and try any of it."

"Don't even think about going back early, or even thinking about work very much," said Anna. "You can spend this time making plans for your own health. Start getting rid of the 20 kilograms first – then you can worry about getting rid of the 20 per cent of costs."

Charlie laughed. "I hadn't thought about it like that, but

there's a nice symmetry there: 20 and 20. I need to trim the same amount of fat from myself as I do from the factory."

There was a flurry of noise and movement as two children flew through the back door, dropped school bags on the floor and headed for the kitchen, calling "Hi Mum. Hi Dad," as they did so.

"Thanks for picking your little sister up from school, Jack," said Anna.

"He was talking to a girl," said Sophie with a grin.

"Be quiet," said Jack.

Realizing that her father was home, Sophie changed direction and headed for Charlie's briefcase.

"What are you looking for, Sophie?" asked Charlie. "I'm afraid you won't find any chocolates in there today."

He smiled at Anna. "And there probably won't be any for a while. It would do all of us good — but especially your dad — to leave all the chocolate at work for a while."

Sophie's face dropped and she headed for the fridge instead.

2   Back to Work

After two weeks of enforced rest Charlie was more than ready to return to work. The day before, he put in a call to his factory manager.

"Charlie. I'm glad you called," said Peter. "I have Antonio with me so I'm going to put you on speaker. He's keen to discuss our target."

After a short pause Antonio's voice could be heard with the distance that comes from a speaker-phone conversation. "How are you Charlie?"

Charlie explained that, on doctor's orders, he'd been doing very little. He described the plan he'd been given by the doctor and joked about the nice mirroring of his 20 kilogram target with Antonio's 20 per cent cost reduction.

"I don't want to be flippant about this," said Antonio, "but I can tell you that if your doctor is saying your weight loss is critical to your survival, he's pretty much exactly describing the situation here. We are being hammered on all sides by globalization. On the one hand imports are getting cheaper while customers are getting more price conscious. On the other hand our export markets are constantly under threat for similar reasons. It's really only our reputation for quality that's keeping us afloat at the moment, but that's not going to be enough in future. On top of those two threats is a third: a couple of private equity firms have been circling, looking at our financials and seeing the potential to make a quick profit through a speedy takeover, stripping out of costs and then reselling the business. Believe me, if that were to happen it wouldn't be pretty. I know that sounds very gloomy, but I want to make the point that maintaining the status quo is not an option. The directors are nervous, and I need to prove to them that you guys have the ability to reduce your costs. That's why I need a plan, and then I need results."

"Understood, Antonio," said Charlie. "It's not going to be easy, but given all the time I've had to think, I do have some ideas. I won't go through them over the phone, but rest assured I'll be working on this with Peter and my team as soon as I get back. We will have a plan for you in two weeks."

"Sounds good," said Antonio.

"Thanks Charlie," said Peter. "We'll leave you to enjoy your last day of rest and I look forward to seeing you in the morning."

* * *

The next morning as Charlie got out of his car it was still quite dark. The unmistakable smell of chocolate filled his lungs and gave him the very strong sense of being back at his second 'home'.

Charlie didn't always attend the planning meeting held early each day. He tried to get there at least once a week, but in the couple of months prior to his heart attack his workload had become so heavy that he hadn't managed to get there at all. He had decided that on this day he would drop in to get a feel for what was going on. Walking into the meeting room, he braced himself for a chorus of "Welcome back!" But there was no such chorus — there was only one person in the room.

"Charlie!" Yu greeted her boss with a wide smile and a hug. "It's great to see you. You've been missed."

They chatted for a few minutes before Charlie had to

ask Yu where everybody else was. "Doesn't this meeting start at 6.30?"

"It's supposed to," said Yu, "though lately everyone hasn't been here until about quarter to. I just use the time to go over my schedule for the day."

Jerry appeared at the door. "Not starting yet? I'll be back in a few minutes. I'll just go and see what happened overnight in the engineering shop. Good to see you back, Charlie," he waved as he hurried off.

Martin came in next with two other team leaders. He acknowledged Charlie and asked after his health, then slumped down into a chair, slamming a wad of papers onto the desk. "That afternoon shift are hopeless. Can't even read a plan. The choc button line was running well so they figured they'd just keep it going on the milk chocolate. They've made five extra bulk bins of stock that we don't need, and haven't changed over to the dark that we desperately need."

Charlie sat silently as Martin, Yu and a number of team leaders joined in a conversation that was half complaining and half blaming, but didn't seem to resolve anything. Halfway through, Jerry re-entered the room and joined in. The conversation then veered in another direction.

"Jerry, what happened on the Number 3 wrapper

yesterday?" said Martin. "You said it would be down for half an hour and we didn't get back on there for the rest of the shift. That fitter you had on there didn't seem to know what he was doing."

"Well if the machine wasn't such a mess, we might have had a chance to do it quickly. But the mess underneath it meant it took a lot longer to pull apart than we thought."

"That would be right," said Martin. "Always blame the operator. If you did a bit of preventative maintenance from time to time maybe there wouldn't be so many broken bags and we'd have less mess to clean up."

"And when are we supposed to do that?" said Jerry. "We're already working excess overtime."

"Whoa, whoa, whoa! That's enough you two." Charlie could stay out of it no longer. With the clarity that comes from time away he could suddenly see a lack of maturity and focus in his team that he hadn't noticed before. He had intended taking a 'softly softly' approach in his first week back; now he realized that if there was going to be any chance of achieving the sort of cuts Antonio and Peter were asking for, he would have to put a firm hand on the reins sooner rather than later.

"All I've heard this morning is blame. Day shift blaming

afternoon shift, production blaming maintenance. It seems to me that everyone is losing sight of the big picture."

There was a pause, then Martin spoke. "And what big picture would that be, Charlie? The vision and mission and all that? I don't think any of us would be able to tell you what they are, and we sure haven't had time to read them while you've been away. No offence, but it's been busy around here." There was a murmur of agreement around the room. Martin managed a half-smile. "Have you gone all philosophical in your down time?"

"Very funny, Martin. But seriously, vision and mission are part of it, but they're not what I'm getting at. Why are we here? What's the main reason we do what we do every day?" As Charlie looked around the room all he could see at this point were blank stares.

"To make chocolate?" someone asked quietly.

"Yes, but we don't just make chocolate for the sake of it."

"To make chocolate for our customers?" said Yu.

"That's right," said Charlie. "In the end, the customer is everything. The customer pays our wages. The customer justifies our existence. And at the moment, I can tell you that our customers are looking elsewhere."

"What do you mean by that?" asked Jerry.

Charlie described his conversation the previous day with Antonio and Peter. "The world we work in is changing, and the only way to survive is to change with it."

"But we're still profitable aren't we?" said Martin. "We see the results – the company is still making good money. And you said yourself that our quality is what separates us from the rest. They won't be able to close that gap very easily. People love our chocolate."

"Sometimes you have to change before you need to," said Charlie. "Have you ever heard of the 'Frys' chocolate brand? I was reading about them in my time off. They were the world's biggest chocolate manufacturer in the mid-1800s. They dwarfed start-up companies like Cadbury's. Seventy years later, Cadbury's took over Fry's and all that survives of that company now are a couple of chocolate bars that still bear their name. Cadbury's ultimate success came because they continued to improve what they were doing while Fry's stuck rigidly to the way they had always done things.

"And I can give you another example." Charlie pointed at himself. "Two weeks ago I had a heart attack. Was that a surprise? Not really. For years my wife and my doctor have been telling me that I needed to change my ways, but I just figured I was okay so I could keep going as I was. I was lucky – very lucky – in that I've been given a second chance. But I won't make it unless I can trim some of this fat off. And what Antonio is saying is that if we don't act now and start trimming some of the fat out of this business, it could come to a sudden, fatal stop as well."

As Charlie looked around the table he was met by silence.

"I know what you're thinking," he said after a short while, half smiling and half smirking. "You're looking at me thinking, *It's okay for him to talk about losing weight – he's got plenty to lose …*" The mood lightened as muffled laughter circled the room. "*But this factory doesn't have so much spare fat – it's running pretty lean already. Am I right?*"

There were half-nods all around the table. Charlie could tell that his team wanted to agree but were being polite about doing so with too much enthusiasm.

"Well," Charlie continued, "there is probably more fat around here than we think, and our mission is going to be to find it."

* * *

A few minutes after the meeting, Yu appeared at the door of Charlie's office. He beckoned her in.

"I'm sorry to burden you with this on your first day back, but I'm a bit worried, Charlie. Working here used to be fun. Heck, it should be fun — most people would kill to work in a chocolate factory. But lately it just seems like everyone's at the end of their tether. You saw what Martin and Jerry were like this morning — that's pretty much the same every day. It's just the degree that varies. And now with this cost thing …"

"I know they've always had a tendency to bicker. They're like an old married couple at times, aren't they?" said Charlie, drawing a smile from Yu. "But if this morning is typical it does seem to have got worse. And anyway, it sounds like you think it is a wider problem than just Martin and Jerry?"

Yu looked down at her lap for a while, then back at Charlie. "I think we're lacking direction. Even before your heart attack, it had got to the stage that we didn't see you much. You always seemed to be in meetings, while we were pretty much left to our own devices. That's fine to a point — I think we all appreciate being trusted — but eventually we start to focus only on what's going on today. On fire fighting, as they say. I think we've lost our sense of purpose – we're just stumbling ahead."

Charlie lifted himself out of his seat and sat on the edge of the desk. "Thank you for your honesty, Yu, and your thoughtfulness. I appreciate them both. I think you're probably right about the lack of purpose and that's something that I have been thinking about. Let me tell you: Martin was actually quite right – I did get a bit philosophical during my time off. Nearly dying tends to do that to you. Which is why I made that point at the end of the meeting – about the need to change even when there is no immediate reason to change."

"Well, maybe this 'fat trimming' scheme, as you put it so vividly, will give us some purpose again. I must go, but thank you for listening, Charlie."

◊ ◊ ◊

"So we're going to walk rather than drink?" said Jason, Charlie's best friend, over the phone.

"Yes, my friend, that's what I said. If you want to catch up with me, that's going to have to be the deal," said Charlie.

"Okay. I can come to terms with that ... I think. I'll see

you at your place after work then. The heady world of banking is surprisingly calm today so I shouldn't be too late."

So it was that after Charlie finished his first day back, he found himself exercising with Jason – something they hadn't done for a long time.

"Probably 20 years," said Jason. "I reckon the last time we went for a walk together – for the sake of the walk – was before your wedding. I remember you were very nervous, so as best man I saw it as my duty to try and relax you."

Charlie laughed. "Well, now you can make it your duty as my best mate to try and keep me to my exercise regime."

"Tell me what the doctor has planned for you."

Charlie described the doctor's plan. It involved a strict diet – there seemed to be a lot of lettuce involved, and nothing remotely fattening. With Anna overseeing things, there was little chance of his veering from the diet – except at work, of course. It was going to take a lot of self-discipline to keep his hands out of the bulk bins. And then there was the exercise. Initially it was mainly regular walking and possibly cycling, with the length of his sessions increasing over time. Later, when he had regained a basic level of fitness, there would be more strenuous exercise – that hadn't been planned yet.

"I have to record everything," said Charlie. "Everything I eat, and everything I do."

"Well, I suppose he wants to keep you honest," said Jason.

"Partly that, but he also wants me to be able to see my progress. By tracking what I do, especially with exercise, he says I'll be able to look back later and marvel at how far I've come."

"Well my friend, if you want someone by your side through all of this, I'm here. Lord knows, I could do with the exercise myself. It's got to be better for us than sitting in the pub."

"Thanks, Jason. I would appreciate the company."

They walked in silence for a while before Jason said, "What about the stress side of things? Anna told me you need to reduce that too, and of course a lot of that comes from work. What are you doing to reduce the pressure there?"

Charlie described his first day back, telling Jason about the cost-reduction target imposed by Antonio, the low morale and arguing amongst his staff, and the 'trim the fat' analogy he had introduced.

Jason looked concerned. "Sounds to me like things

have got worse, not better," he said.

"Yes, by the end of the day I was thinking the same thing," said Charlie. "Yu, my best team leader, suggested to me that the cost-cutting goal might give the team some direction, but I'm not so sure. I just wonder whether they are ready to tackle a big project."

Having reached the top of a short rise in the path, Charlie stopped and leaned back on a wall, breathing heavily. After a few minutes he was breathing more normally again and continued.

"Anna wants me to delegate more, to share the load of this cost-cutting exercise. I'm not sure they're ready for that either. I think I need to work on the morale first – to get them back on side – before giving them more responsibility. But I don't have time for that. So yes, it is stressful."

They stopped at an intersection to wait for the Walk signal.

"For what it's worth, I think Anna's right," said Jason. "From what you've told me in the past, you have a lot experience in that leadership team, don't you? I suspect you'll find they're capable of taking on more than you think. And giving them a 'stretch goal', as our sales guys like to call it, would certainly take their minds off fighting with each other."

27

"I guess you're right," said Charlie as they started walking again.

"Call a meeting, make a plan together and get going. It doesn't sound to me like you have much time to waste if you're going to keep the bosses happy. You can do it, Charlie – if anyone can, you can."

Charlie thanked his friend for the vote of confidence, then changed the subject as they headed for home.

* * *

When Charlie arrived home Jack was waiting for him. "Have you seen my tennis racquet, Dad?" he said. "I've been asked to make up a group tomorrow night."

"Have they ever seen you play tennis?" asked Charlie with raised eyebrows.

"It's purely social," smiled Jack. "Mixed doubles."

"Say no more," said Charlie with a wink. "I think I saw your racquet in the shed. I'll have a look."

Charlie opened the shed door and groaned to himself at the mess he was confronted with. Nevertheless, it took him only a few minutes to spot his son's racquet. As he pulled it off the shelf he noticed an old dumbbell set on the same shelf – a relic from a get-fit scheme quite a few years earlier. He leaned over to pull it out too ... and immediately felt a sharp pain in his back.

3 Plan

"What were you planning to do with the weights in the first place?" asked the doctor as he felt around Charlie's back.

"I don't know, Doc. I thought they might help me get my strength back, if I took it carefully."

"All in good time, Charlie," said the doctor. "But there is a reason why we haven't talked about strength in your health plan yet: you've got to take it one step at a time.

"Your body is a system, and you have to work on it with that in mind. So the *plan* is about rebuilding some basic fitness by losing weight through diet and fairly light exercise. Your job is to *do* that — to take those actions and nothing more. Later, when our *checks* reveal that you're making good progress on your initial weight-loss target of 20 kilograms, and your cardiology tests are showing that your heart's condition has improved, then we can *adjust* your plan and introduce other forms of exercise and improvement in things like strength. When we get to that point I'll let you dust off those dumbbells if you like, but for now I'd like you to leave them in the shed."

Charlie nodded. "Stick to the plan," he said.

"Stick to the plan," said the doctor. "Now, let's check your weight and blood pressure. I don't think you've hurt your back badly – just a slight strain. If it gives you too much trouble I'll send you to a physio, but let's wait and see for a few days."

* * *

Charlie stood in front of his team, waiting until he had their full attention. It made him feel like a schoolteacher. Eventually they quietened down and looked at him.

"It's now 10 past 10. Our meeting was scheduled to start at 10. We used to start our meetings on time and I'm the first to admit that I've let our standards slip. But it's time to reset the clock. Martin, how many of us are in this room?"

Martin looked around and answered, "Twelve".

"So how much time have we wasted in total in the last 10 minutes?"

Martin looked blank so Charlie looked around for someone else to answer. Yu called out, "One hundred and twenty minutes."

"That's right, Yu. Think about that everyone: we've collectively spent two hours of our time waiting for a meeting to start. And that's just one meeting. Think about how much time that would add up to over all the meetings we have, including the daily planning meeting."

Charlie turned to the whiteboard behind him and did a quick calculation. He hadn't planned on pursuing this point so far, but it was turning out to be quite powerful.

---

10 minutes x 12 people = 2 hours

2 hours x 10 meetings/week = 20 hrs/wk

"At the very least it would be 20 hours a week. Now I don't know off the top of my head how much that time is worth in dollars, though we could work it out. But if I said to you, Martin, that I want to give Yu a couple of days off and that I want you to cover for her as well as doing your normal job, how would you feel?"

Martin's look negated the need for an answer.

"Exactly. None of us has that much time to waste, yet we waste it all the time. Now, the other day I drew a parallel between waste in our factory and the 'waste' – excess fat – that I am carrying around. If we think of our waste as 'fat', then we've just proved that there is at least some fat that could be trimmed from this business. And my guess is that there is plenty more where that came from."

Charlie wasn't surprised that the faces in front of him showed varying levels of understanding. Lowering his voice for effect, he said: "From now on, our meetings will start on time. When I call a meeting for 10, we will start at 10 no matter who is in the room. If you arrive late, don't expect to be brought up to speed. This wasted meeting time will be the first piece of fat we trim from our business. Any objections?" Silence and shaking heads followed.

"Now, on to the purpose of this meeting, which is about

how we are going to trim a substantial amount of fat from this business."

Charlie turned to the whiteboard behind him and wrote '20' on it in large digits.

"This is the magic number." In more detail than he had provided at the last meeting, he described the conversation he'd been having with Peter and Antonio. He explained the increasing pressure from imports, the price pressure on exports and the potential threat from share market raiders. "Let me explain that last point. Put simply, if an investment company thinks that our costs are high relative to our profits, it makes us a takeover target. They see an opportunity to come in, cut costs quickly – usually by sacking a lot of staff – then resell the company at a higher price. It's like seeing an old chair on eBay that you buy, clean up and resell.

"The bottom line is that we need to cut our costs, across the plant, by 20 per cent over the next year. And we need to show management a plan to do this in two weeks."

"Twenty per cent!" said a number of the team at once. "In a year?"

The meeting broke into a number of conversations, the group clearly having trouble digesting the task in front of them. Charlie let them go for a minute then called for order.

"We can carry on all we like," said Charlie, "but sometimes we just have to face harsh realities. Believe me, when my doctor told me recently that I have to lose 20 kilograms I felt the same as you do now. But then I came to understand that he wasn't setting me that goal for the sake of it — he was doing it to keep me alive. Antonio and Peter are setting us this goal for pretty much the same reason — to keep this factory alive."

Some heated discussion followed, with various accusations about the bosses being out of touch with reality, arbitrary numbers plucked out of the air and defense of all the hard work that everyone was already putting in to their work. Charlie did his best to stay calm, batting back each objection with the best answer he could offer.

Eventually he held up both hands, palms toward the group.

"Look, the main reason this goal seems so big is that we're looking at it as a whole: as one big number in one short timeframe. We need to think of it like a diet — and I'm paraphrasing my doctor here. We're not going to trim all the fat out of this place in one go. What we need to do is break the challenge down into smaller, manageable 'mini-goals'. Then I think we'll start to see how the task is not as unrealistic as you all think."

"Why don't we just cut our labor numbers across the board?" said Jerry. "Wouldn't that be the most straightforward way to do this? Or we could scrap a couple of the less profitable products and trim down the afternoon shift."

"Because those sorts of approach rarely work," said Charlie. "They inevitably lead to cutting expenditure that actually does add value — that makes a profitable contribution — while leaving in place other expenditure that is unnecessary and/or unprofitable. It's for precisely those reasons that we're going to go in almost the opposite direction."

"We could replace our excuse for a computer system, which constantly seems to be breaking down," said Martin.

"I'd also like to know what reductions will be made outside the factory — in the office, and in the warehouses?" added Jerry.

"As you know, the system is under review, but it is just one tool and it has less effect on our efficiency than you think. And yes, Jerry, other areas of the business are also being asked to cut their costs too. The point here is that we need to focus our energy and efforts on those things that we can control."

Wanting to avoid the conversation diverging into all the negatives again, Charlie carried straight on.

"The first thing we're going to do is to slice this project up like a cake so that everyone has their own piece to work with." Acknowledging with a laugh that cake was probably not the best analogy to use when talking about a diet, he pressed on. "I know that you all have good ideas about how you could improve your areas. I want each of you to work with your team to find those improvements, to come up with a plan to trim some fat from your section, and then to come back to me and tell me what contribution your team can make to the overall 20 per cent cost-reduction goal. In this way, we take the least efficient expenditure in each department and target that. And, better still, you and your people, who know your areas better than anyone else, are the ones who choose where the cuts will come from."

Charlie said that there were two main tools they could use to help guide their decision making.

"The first tool is our profit and loss statement, otherwise known as the 'P and L' or simply 'PNL'. In some places they also call this an 'income statement'." Charlie handed copies of a single sheet of paper around the room. The sheet was a table with a lot of numbers in it. "How many of you have seen this before?"

"I haven't seen ours," said Martin, "but my father ran

Profit and Loss (PNL) Statement

For the period July 2010 to June 2011

	$
Income/Revenue	
Bar line sales	5,425,200
Molded product sales	3,256,000
Assortment sales	4,500,500
Total revenue	13,181,700
Expenses/Costs	
Raw materials	4,560,500
Direct labor	5,480,500
Total cost of sales	10,041,000
Administration	800,500
Maintenance	601,200
Building leases	80,000
Information Technology	55,000
Total expenses	11,577,700
Net profit	**1,604,000**

his own mechanics business and petrol station. He used to show me how the profit and loss worked. In the top section it has our income, which for us is the money earned from product sales. And in the bottom section it has our expenses: how much is spent in each area over the period of the chart."

"Great, Martin. While this table might look complicated, it's actually pretty simple. So if we take maintenance, for instance, the table shows expenditure of $600,000. As this is the PNL for the last year, that's how much was spent in the maintenance department over that year."

"So all I need to do is cut that by $120,000," said Jerry. "That'll be easy. Martin, you don't need any preventative maintenance done this year do you?"

"Enough of the sarcasm, Jerry. I'll make two points. First, this is the total aggregated number, so in some ways for your department it is not much better than the company-wide number − or my 20 kilograms, for that matter. I'll give you a more detailed expense breakdown for your department, showing exactly where the money goes in terms of wages, overtime, consumables and so on. From that you'll be able to focus on those areas with the greatest potential. Second, the 20 per cent goal is a shared goal. If one department can find more than that, your area might not need to cut so deep. That means that it's in everyone's interest to help everyone else, and you should look at how you can work together with some of your colleagues to make joint savings. The worst thing we can do is make this a competition in which you all look after your own area at the expense of everyone else."

Charlie paused, pulled a seat toward him and sat down. "When I distribute the more detailed PNL after this meeting, you'll all get all of it. The idea is that everyone looks for savings everywhere. If you see a potential saving in another department, or which you could make in your department by changing something in another department, talk to them about it. But when you come back to me with your plan, I want to know what contribution your area is going to make to our savings target."

"Isn't this a bit limiting, Charlie?" said Martin. "I know one thing my dad was always talking about was the waste that didn't appear in the PNL. Like when I worked for him in the school holidays and was a bit slow serving customers."

"You mean you actually served customers?" said a younger voice.

"Yes, back in those days we did. Anyway, if I was too slow, and the queue got too long, Dad figured that potential customers would just keep driving past and go to the next petrol station. That lost business wouldn't show up in the PNL."

"You're quite right Martin. While your example is a waste of revenue, rather than expense, there are likely plenty of both that won't appear explicitly on the PNL. It should be seen as a starting point, but you should encourage your teams to look for any form of waste – not just that which will appear in a line on the financials. That's why the second tool you have to help you with your project is these." He pointed the middle and index fingers of his right hand at his eyes. "You need to learn how to use these properly, and to teach your team members to do the same."

Uncomprehending looks came from around the room.

"To demonstrate, I want you to follow me downstairs onto the floor." With that, Charlie stood up and moved towards the door. Slowly, the group stood up behind him and followed. As Charlie led his team out, he could tell that he was a way off having everyone 'sold' on his plan of dividing up the work, but at least they had stopped complaining about the impossibility of it all. Reality was starting to sink in.

* * *

Down in the factory Charlie found a space out of the road of forklift traffic and gathered his team around him.

"While I was at home recuperating over the last two weeks, I was doing a lot of reading. One particular article I read struck me as really interesting. It talked about an approach used in a Japanese factory to induct a new manager. The manager was taken down to the factory floor by a trainer. He was asked to stand inside a circle that had been marked on the floor in the center of the plant. The trainer then left him there, without any instructions other than that he was to stay inside the circle, telling him he would return. After a couple of hours, the trainer returned and asked the new manager what he had learnt, to which the manager replied incredulously, 'You're kidding — how could I learn anything while I've been standing in this circle waiting for you to come back?'"

"Two hours? That seems a bit over the top," said Jerry.

"It doesn't really matter — the point is it was a long time," said Charlie. "Anyway, the trainer told the manager that he was not yet ready, then went away again, leaving the manager in his circle. After another hour of standing inside the circle, getting increasingly bored, the manager started to pass the time by looking around at what everyone was doing in the factory. He started to notice small things: an operator handling sensitive materials without gloves; a machine that had stopped and remained idle, seemingly unnoticed, for over half an hour; another operator who was double- and triple-handling parts as he went about his work.

"When the trainer eventually returned, he again asked the manager what he had learnt. The manager replied that he still hadn't learnt much, but shared with the trainer what he had noticed. To this, the trainer replied, 'You have learnt something very important: you have learnt to *see*.'"

Charlie waited, looking at the group in front of him to gauge whether his message had got through.

"That's a good story, Charlie, but I don't see the relevance to us," said Jerry. "All of us have been here for quite a long time. I've worked here for over 18 years. There isn't much here that I don't see."

"I think you might be surprised, Jerry. What we all tend to do is rush around all day, putting out our various fires. We rarely, if ever, stop to look at what is going on in our department. Occasionally something will go wrong and that will cause some sort of wasteful or unsafe practice to come to our attention; what we don't notice is those wasteful or unsafe practices *before* they cause a big problem.

"It's a bit like the diet they've put me on. I have to re-cord everything I eat, which really makes me aware of what I'm eating. All of a sudden the odd biscuit here, the odd slice of cheese there − stuff that I was eating out of habit more than need − it's all much more obvious. In the factory we can pick up some of that in the numbers, but a lot more of it by taking the time to see what is really going on.

"According to the article, we need to learn to see at what the Japanese call *gemba*." Charlie spelt out the word. "What that means is going to where the action is and seek-ing the facts. It applies to problem solving, but also to this idea of actually looking at what is going on. Mostly it means, for those of us who spend a lot of time in meetings, that we need to make the effort to spend as much time as we can on the factory floor."

"Something I've noticed lately," said Yu, "is that one of my people will come to me with a suggestion. Usually, because my mind is on something else, I write down their suggestion in my notebook ... and that's the last thing that happens to it. I guess that part of what you're saying is that we need to take the time to stop and look at what they are suggesting − to really hear it as well as see it."

"Good point, Yu. That's important for a couple of

reasons. An ignored suggestion might be a lost opportunity. But also, after a few ignored suggestions your people will stop making them — in effect they will lose the ability to see as well."

Charlie looked at his watch. "Okay everyone, we need to wrap this meeting up. Later today I'll bring the detailed PNLs around and work through them with each of you. With your teams, I want you to work with those, and these," he said pointing to his eyes again, "and come up with a cost-cutting plan by this time in two days. It's Wednesday today, so we'll meet upstairs again as a group on Friday morning at 10. What time?"

"Ten!" they said in unison.

"Yes, on the dot. Any questions in the meantime, come and see me." Charlie clasped his hands together. "I have faith in all of you. I know we can do this. Let's put this factory on a diet!"

* * *

Feeling quite pleased with the way his meeting had gone, Charlie called into Peter's office on the way back to his own. As he walked into the room he noticed that something was different. The room seemed darker. Then he noticed a blind drawn over the window that looked down onto the factory floor. He asked Peter about it.

"To be honest," said Peter, "I find the chaos of the factory floor a bit stressful. Every time I look out there I see people wandering around aimlessly. There seems to be so much time spent looking for other people, or looking for stock. I can't believe how often the packing machines stop while operators hunt around the floor for the right bulk bin so they can get going again. It's so unproductive."

Charlie couldn't help but laugh, which caused Peter to look at him quizzically. Charlie described the meeting they'd just had, including his plan to slice the cost-cutting project up amongst his team, and how he had described the *gemba* concept and the importance of 'seeing'. "Perhaps I should bring the team up here to your office and get them to look out your window. It seems that you're doing more seeing than they are."

Peter moved over to the window and drew the blind open again. "I'm not sure about that," he said, "but if there are going to be positive changes down there I want to see them too. Thanks for the reality check — it is important to stay in touch, isn't it."

* * *

Later in the day Charlie was taking a walk around the factory before heading home. As he turned a corner into the warmth of the chocolate manufacturing room, Martin beckoned him over towards his office.

"Do you have a minute, Charlie?"

"Of course, Martin. What is it?"

They sat on either side of Martin's desk. Just as Martin was about to speak, one of his supervisors came to the door.

"Tim?"

"Sorry Martin, but do you have the afternoon shift schedule?"

Martin spent some time rifling through papers on his desk before coming up with a schedule. Tim was about to leave when he paused, pointing out that he had been given the wrong program – Martin had given him an earlier provisional schedule rather than the finalized version. After a couple of minutes more searching Martin finally came up with the correct schedule. He asked Tim to close the door as he left.

Martin turned back to Charlie. "I'm really not happy about this cost-cutting target. I've been working here a long time, and I can't for the life of me see how we're going to cut 20 per cent out of our expenses. It's too big an ask. We're already working as hard as we can – harder than I remember working before – and just keeping our heads above water."

Charlie sighed. "The problem is, Martin, that we don't really have a choice. I wasn't making up that stuff about market pressures and takeover threats. The world has changed. It sounds morbid, but it really is a parallel situation to my own. If I don't lose weight I could die; if this factory doesn't lose weight it could die. And believe me, when the doctor first said to me that I needed to lose 20 kilograms I almost laughed in his face. But when he explained that that was about a kilogram every two weeks, it suddenly seemed achievable. We need to think in a similar way here: don't see it as one big challenge, but rather a whole lot of small ones."

"But then there's the time issue. I don't know where I'm going to find the time to plan these cuts, let alone implement them."

"Why do you think I asked all of you to go away, find the 'fat' and come back to me with a plan?" asked Charlie.

"Because you thought we were best placed to see the fat, as you call it?" said Martin.

"Partly that, yes. But partly because I realized that I

needed to spread the load — I couldn't do all this myself. And surely both of those things are true for you too. Your team — the folks who spend all their time on the floor doing the work — are best placed to find the waste, and they can share the load with you while they look for it."

"Well I guess so," said Martin. "Though they'll all claim that they are busy too."

"Sometimes — often — busyness doesn't equate to efficiency. Before we started this chat, how much time did you spend looking around for the schedule Tim was asking for?"

Martin guessed a couple of minutes, which Charlie then doubled because he had had to do it twice. Charlie calculated that in total Martin probably spent 20 to 30 minutes a week just looking for paper, with which Martin couldn't disagree.

---

2 minutes x 2 searches = 4 minutes

4 min x 6-7 times/wk = 24-28 min/wk

"And if Tim hadn't noticed that he had been given the provisional program, and had gone on to run that program, how much time would have been spent tomorrow correcting the results of that? Probably the whole day; am I right?"

Martin nodded.

"It's not only fat out there on the floor that we need to be trimming. It's also fat in here, and in everything that we do. There are opportunities everywhere if we look for them."

As Charlie stood up to leave, he said: "Let me give you a free kick. If you want to save some of that 30 minutes a week, go down and see what Yu does with her production schedules."

Martin still wasn't looking convinced but he reluctantly agreed to try and come up with a plan by the Friday meeting.

* * *

Over the next day Charlie watched from his office window, and walked around the plant, observing his team leaders bringing their teams together to make cost-cutting plans. A few times he was asked to join a meeting and explain the background to the cost-cutting target and why it was needed, how the detailed PNL numbers worked, or how some form of identified waste actually related to the financials. More than once an operator exclaimed that he or she had had no idea how much money was being spent in one area or another. "We spend that much on cleaning products?" "That much money is spent on packaging waste!"

Charlie was also invited to give a few groups his *gemba* story about the new manager being asked to stand in a circle for hours. Aside from a few jokes from operators wishing they could get their supervisor to stay in a circle all day, most seemed to get the message. All agreed that after a while they probably stopped really 'seeing' what was going on around them.

In general Charlie was pleasantly surprised by the positive tone of the discussions, though he did recall that quite often in the past he had had operators bursting at the seams with ideas just waiting to come out. He looked forward to what his team leaders would bring him the next day.

* * *

Charlie walked into the meeting just before 10 on the Friday morning and found a room full of people. It was an encouraging sign. He wasted no time getting started.

"Okay everyone, today is the day we make our plan to put this factory on a diet. Cost reductions of 20 per cent — that's the big goal. Now let's hear about how you and your teams intend to contribute towards achieving it. Who would like to start?"

Yu stood up and went to the front of the room. She distributed copies of her team's plan, showing before and after versions of the PNL statement for the hand-packing area. Being a labor-intensive area of the factory, where individual chocolates were placed into assortment boxes on a production line, it was clear that more efficient use of labor needed to be her major goal. She outlined some initiatives they thought they could take in the area, including some rearrangement of the layout. She had also estimated costs associated with making the changes.

"We won't know until we see what happens when we've made the changes," Yu said, "but our initial estimate is that we should be able to cut the costs in our area by at least the 20 per cent we committed to — and quite quickly. Most of that will be a reduction in labor, which will be achieved mainly by using fewer casual workers, which will lead to further savings in training costs as we spend quite a lot training those casuals. I've also talked to Martin and we'll be able to redeploy a couple of our permanent staff to his area, again reducing casual labor costs. The rearrangement should also lead to reduced work-in-progress inventory levels and some other associated cost savings."

Charlie thanked Yu for her thoroughness.

Over the next two hours each of Charlie's team leaders stood up and presented their section's cost-cutting plan. Some of the team surprised him with what they had come up with. Others disappointed a little. Despite the talk with Martin, the chocolate manufacturing and molding plan was quite light on detail and only identified potential savings of 12 per cent. This was well under where he needed to be, given his area had the highest proportion of costs overall – he really needed to be somewhere close to 20 per cent, regardless of what other areas did. Jerry peppered his presentation with negative comments along the lines of, "We've tried all these things before and none of them worked" and "We're doing what we can". However, he did present, if a bit begrudgingly, potential savings of 18 per cent. A positive of Jerry's presentation was that around half his savings had been identified by working with other sections on ways of reducing changeover times on various machines.

As Jerry sat down, Martin asked him whether his cuts would have any effect on preventative maintenance. "Not a strong point at the moment, before the cuts, I would say."

Jerry didn't take the bait. He remained calm and said that in fact they were currently 30 days behind schedule on preventative maintenance, but with the plan they had made he had held back enough hours to catch that up over six months.

"That's great, Jerry," said Charlie. "If you can pull that off it is bound to reduce downtime and all the costs associated with it."

At the end of the session Charlie went to the whiteboard and did a quick sum of the savings estimated by each group. He pecked away at his calculator for a few minutes then wrote "19%" on the whiteboard.

"Well," he said, "by the look of this we're very close to where we need to be. I reckon that if we're able to hit this number, we'll probably find the extra one per cent along the way as well. Come to think of it, if I lost 19 kilograms I'd feel like I was really on a roll and easily go on to lose one more. Well done everyone – it looks like we have a plan."

As the meeting wrapped up and his team disbursed, Charlie reflected further on the target. He really wasn't worried about that extra 1 per cent. Deep down he knew that the positive energy for change that would come out of hitting 19 per cent would be more than enough to carry along the stragglers. People like Martin would find it much harder to be pessimistic if surrounded by enthusiasm and real results, and would probably outstrip their original predictions as a result.

Charlie headed home happy that progress was being made.

○ ○ ○

The next week ran relatively smoothly as Charlie left his team to start implementing their plans. He spent some time working from home as he compiled his team's various plans in a form that he could present to the directors on the Friday afternoon.

"Could you help me with some of my homework please Dad," said Sophie after dinner on the Thursday night. "I've got so much to do I don't know where to start."

"I have an idea," said Charlie. He went to his bag and pulled out a chocolate bar. "If I gave you this chocolate bar, would you eat it all in one bite?"

"No, of course not," laughed Sophie. "That would make me choke."

"So how would you eat it?"

"I'd break a piece off one end and eat that. Then break off another piece, and so on."

"Exactly," said Charlie. "So what if I gave you this bar and said you can eat one piece of chocolate after each piece of homework that you finish?"

"Then …" Sophie's eyes lit up in recognition. "I get what you're saying! I need to break my homework up into chunks too, don't I?"

Charlie smiled and handed Sophie the chocolate. "Well, off you go then."

Moving over to join his wife, Charlie slumped down into the sofa.

"We're looking good," he said. He took her through his report and the range of plans his team leaders had come up with. "I feel like we've got the 'P' of your 'PDCA' cycle pretty well nailed down. I've talked it through with Peter and Antonio and we're ready to take it to the directors' meeting."

After chatting for a while, Charlie announced that he was off to bed. "I know I have to lose some weight and get fit, but I wish that didn't involve getting up before the birds for a walk."

"Ah, well," said Anna, patting Charlie's leg, "that's where

things are going to get harder at work too. Your *Plan* is no good without *Do* as well."

"Touché," said Charlie. As he stood up his mobile phone rang. Charlie looked at the clock: 10pm. A frown creased his face as he picked up the phone and saw the number of his quality manager on its screen.

4 Do

It was approaching midnight by the time Charlie parked his car. This, he felt, was not what his doctor meant by reducing his stress levels.

He walked through the darkened office area and down to the factory floor. Down there, the bright lighting gave lie to the fact that outside these walls most of the city was sleeping.

Charlie strode across the factory to the warehouse, noting a strange quiet that resulted from the caramel bar line sitting idle. As he reached the store he met Jerry coming from another direction. They exchanged nods then walked silently to where Mohammed, the quality manager, and Martin stood beside a pallet of cartons.

Mohammed explained the problem. "One of my team was doing a random check of this product and discovered a number of underweight bars. He then opened a few more boxes in other pallets and found even more. Not every bar is under the required weight, but perhaps one in 10, based on this quick check. All the product comes from the batch that was produced this afternoon."

All eyes turned to Martin. "As soon as Mo alerted me to it we stopped the machine. Mo has had the entire batch quarantined. It seems the hot-water lines that warm the enrobers weren't working properly. Some of the nozzles became clogged which, in turn, led to some bars getting a lighter coating of chocolate than they should have. We're now in the process of washing the enrobers out completely. Jerry's guys are working on fixing the hot-water problem."

"And do we have any idea why this wasn't detected?" asked Charlie. "Why didn't the check-weighers on the end of the line alert us to the problem earlier?" Mohammed looked at Jerry, who was avoiding eye contact. "Jerry?"

"We've been having trouble with that check-weigher for a few days. It kept rejecting product that was actually within specification. We were working on it yesterday on day shift but couldn't fix the problem so we turned it off. We organized Mo's people to do extra weight checks, which was fine on day shift – but that message didn't get through to the afternoon shift."

There was silence for a moment before Martin said, "And you decided to keep this to yourself – not to let anyone in management, not Mo or me or Charlie, know about it?"

"I didn't 'decide' not to tell you – I just didn't get around to it. We were under pressure. I had one of your supervisors breathing down my neck because he wanted to meet his production quota. By rights we should have just stopped the machine in the first place."

"Oh, so it's our fault now?" said Martin

"If we could get a reasonable amount of time to work on the machines – if they weren't always running behind schedule ..." said Jerry.

Charlie held his arms in the air. "That'll do. Attributing blame isn't going to get us anywhere. What we have to do now is remove the risk to our customers and get going again as soon as we can." He paused, swallowing what he was about to say. In the past, this was precisely the sort of situation where he would have taken over, effectively relieving his team leaders of the burden. But he wasn't going to do that this time, despite the seriousness of the situation. "So where are we now?"

"I've got two blokes working on the hot-water situation," said Jerry. "They tell me it's under control – they're changing the pump over and will be ready to go for the morning shift. The check-weigher will take longer – we have the supplier coming to see us first thing in the morning but that will be after the shift starts."

"Well as long as we know we can do extra manual checks," said Martin. "And if the enrober is not clogged, there won't be an issue with underweight product anyway."

"What about the finished product, Mo?"

"It will need to be sorted by reweighing and repacking, which is a fair bit of work. But I'm confident we've isolated the product in question before it went out to the market."

"Okay. It sounds to me like you've all taken the necessary action to get both customer risk and production under control. Now, it's late. I suggest that if you're satisfied that you can leave your night-shift teams to get on with their jobs, the four of us go home and get some sleep. Tomorrow we can work on how to stop this happening again. I'll see you – Jerry and Martin – at our meeting in the morning."

* * *

Charlie had scheduled the 'fat trimming' project meeting with his team leaders for 10 o'clock. He wanted to be up to date on their progress before he went into the directors' meeting that afternoon. He knew that some teams were doing better than others, so also thought the meeting might serve as a prod for some of the slower moving departments.

As the meeting was about to start, there were two notable absentees: Martin and Jerry. "Any idea where they are?" he asked the group.

"Something about a quality problem – that's what Martin said to me," said Yu.

Charlie sighed. "Please excuse me everyone while I make a call and chase them up. I know – I said we would start on time regardless – but there's an important point to be made here."

A few minutes later Martin walked in, Jerry close behind him, both looking rough around the edges.

"Martin," said Charlie before the team leader took a seat. "Can you give us a short update on your cost-cutting projects?"

"Give me a break, boss. It's been a hell of a week – fires to put out every day, not least this underweight problem. That's why I wasn't here at 10. So yes, I can give you a short update: the update is that we have done pretty much nothing since the last meeting." Martin sat down heavily.

"Fair enough, Martin. I'm sorry to have put you on the spot." Looking around at the whole team, he said: "But there's an important point to be made here for all of us. Martin is busy. Things go wrong and he finds himself putting out fires every day. And because he cares a great deal about getting things right, he gets personally involved in each one of those problems.

"This is precisely where each of us needs to change our behavior. I'm the first to acknowledge that it's an area that I'm trying to change too. It's why, last night, I left resolving the underweight problem to Martin and Jerry, rather than taking over myself. If we are going to make a real difference to this factory and trim the fat that we need to trim, then each of us needs to develop the ability to stand back and let our people take more responsibility."

Charlie walked over and sat next to Martin. "Martin. How much have you seen of me this morning — how many questions have I asked you about last night's quality problem?"

"None, come to think of it. I haven't seen you until now." said Martin.

Charlie stood up again. "Can I tell you that that has been a deliberate decision on my part? Can I tell you just how hard it has been to keep my nose out of it? But I decided last night that you seemed to have the situation under control and that I would leave you to it. As the caramel bar line was running again when I arrived this morning, that reinforced for me that I had made the right call. In the meantime, I've been spending my time preparing for this meeting and this afternoon's directors' meeting rather than getting in your way."

Charlie explained that this was what they all needed to do more of. Just as they had shared the load with their teams in planning — in identifying possible ways to reduce costs — they also needed to share the load with their teams in the 'doing'. They needed to stand back from time to time, keeping an eye on the progress of their department's *planned* actions, and not get drawn into the detail of every little *unexpected* problem. And they had to have faith in the ability of their people to manage some things on their own.

"Funnily enough, my own health situation has made me realize the importance of this. My doctor and my wife are barracking on the sidelines, but the nature of my challenge is that the actual 'playing' — the action — has to be taken by me. It's my body after all. They have no choice but to let me get on with it. It doesn't mean they don't care, that they're not staying involved and doing what they can to help. But in the end it's up to me. We, as leaders, need to be more like supporters than players."

As the meeting continued and other team leaders described their progress it was clear that Martin was by no means the only one getting pulled off course by day-to-day interruptions. It was only early days – only a week since the groups had set down their plans – but Charlie understood only too well the downsides of allowing daily distractions to get in the way of taking real action. He would have to watch this and continue to reinforce the need for his team to keep focused on the main goal.

The final team leader to speak was Yu. She invited everyone to come down to the packing line so that they could see for themselves what her team had been doing.

As they approached the hand-packing area, Yu walked ahead and waved to one of her operators.

"I'd like Greta to show you what we've done as a lot of it was her idea," said Yu.

Greta, an older lady who Charlie knew only as a quiet, steady worker, smiled nervously. She pointed to a packing station: a narrow conveyer along which plastic inserts for chocolate assortments were carried. Packers spread along the line inserted individual chocolates into the pockets of the inserts, each packer responsible for one type of chocolate.

"We've always had this line set up with an extra person on the end whose job it was to fill any pockets that had been missed as the trays moved along the line. For a while I'd thought this was a bit of a waste. So when Yu raised the topic of cutting costs, I asked if we could do some calculations. We worked out that by slowing the line down by just a small amount – about 10 per cent – the number of missed pockets reduced to almost zero. That meant we could take one person off the line." Greta looked at Yu.

"While the capacity of the line is slightly lower," said Yu, "the productivity per person is higher and our costs are lower. We checked with the production planners. On this line there is plenty of spare capacity, so we thought we'd give it a try."

"Greta," said Charlie. "What happens if a pocket is missed under this new system?"

"The last packer just pulls the tray off the line and puts it aside to deal with before the next break. Because there are so few now, they're easy to handle that way."

Charlie directed his attention to the whole team. "Here you see a great example of what I've been talking about: an idea coming from someone who works on the line, some calculation to test its viability, and then putting it into practice. And the best thing about this improvement is that it is so counterintuitive: slowing down the line to increase productivity."

He turned to Greta and Yu. "Great work," he said.

Yu took the team around the rest of her department and pointed to various other initiatives; some were still being planned but a number were already in place. "What we're doing first is working on a number of small things," she said. "I figured that was a good way of making change without having to try and get the funds to make more expensive changes."

"I can see what Yu and her team have done," said Martin as they headed back upstairs, "but you have to admit that it's easier to do these sorts of things in a manual packing area than on continuous, largely automatic lines like mine. The planners wouldn't be too pleased if I slowed down the bar line — especially after losing a full shift of output last night."

"That's true to some extent, Martin," said Charlie, "though you have manual operations too: storing bulk bins and moving them around, changing over from one product to another, that sort of thing. But the main point here is that Yu's team have had their eyes wide open to possibility. They weren't trying to copy what someone else had done — they were simply looking closely at what they were doing and asking 'Why?' over and over."

Charlie wrapped up the meeting and scheduled another one for the following week. "We've made a start, everyone, no matter how small. I am encouraged." In truth he didn't feel very encouraged, but he was anxious to keep morale up — and Yu's examples had been a great way to finish the meeting.

* * *

Later that afternoon Peter, Antonio and Charlie gathered in Peter's office.

"Well done," said Antonio. "It seems the directors are satisfied with your plans. But of course that is just the start. What we need now is to see some meaningful action. This has to be about more than lip service: we can't wait six months and then discover that nothing has been done because of this, that or the other. The underweight situation is significant on two levels. First, it obviously has unexpected costs associated with it: loss of a shift's production and a number of hours worth of rework and repackaging. Second, it's a warning. Obviously it's a warning about quality, but more than that it's a warning that these sorts of things can easily distract from the main game. A few of them in short succession and you'll find the time has gone but no improvement has been made. I'm going to want frequent updates, but mostly I need you two to follow these plans right through."

"I fully agree," said Charlie. "While some of the costs associated with this problem will fit under the wastage allowance in the budget, reducing that allowance is an important part of the bar line plan. And as for the potential for distractions like this to pull us off course, we had a conversation along those lines only this morning."

"That's good to hear," said Antonio. "I'll leave you to it and look forward to seeing the results."

"I feel like we need something more concrete to keep us on track," Charlie said to Anna that evening. "Your description of how planning is done at your work was really useful, but I'm afraid that if I don't do something different the plans we've made will easily get swamped by day-to-day 'happenings'."

"Oh, we find that pretty easy," said Anna. "The board keeps everyone in touch with what's going on, what progress is being made and what problems are getting in the way."

"The board? What board?" said Charlie. "I don't remember you mentioning a board."

"Didn't I? Sorry. I guess it didn't seem so important when we were talking about planning. The main point I wanted to make there was that our planning approach shares the load — and it sounds like you're achieving that as well. Once the plan has been developed, though, our PDCA board helps keep us on track and also helps everyone keep in touch with what's going on and how we are progressing."

"Tell me more," said Charlie.

"I'll do better," said Anna. "Tomorrow is Saturday so we need to take Sophie to her music lesson in the morning. Why don't we go together and we can drop into my office around the corner while she's there. Then I can show you the board."

"Sounds good," said Charlie. "Now, I'm off for a walk. Can't let all this get in the way of my own action!"

                                  ❂ ❂ ❂

The following Friday morning as Charlie's team walked into the meeting room they were greeted by a large board attached to the wall. After seeing a similar board at Anna's office, Charlie had spent most of this week organizing his own version. The board was covered in charts, lines and each of their names. It generated a quizzical whirr of conversation before Charlie started the meeting, but he refused to be drawn on the many "What's all this about?" questions addressed to him.

At 10 o'clock Charlie acknowledged that he was pleased to see that all his team were in the room.

"Today I want to introduce you to a new member of our team," he said, indicating the board on the wall. "This is our 'PDCA Board'. It is going to keep us honest over the coming months as we work to make this factory more lean."

Charlie paused for effect, but where he had hoped for looks of expectation he was mostly getting back blank stares.

"Before we move to the board, I need to put it into context. Has anyone ever heard of PDCA before? It stands for 'Plan – Do – Check – Adjust'. Has anyone heard of this before?"

"I think we have a poster in the workshop with something like that on it," said Jerry. "It's been there for a long time but I have no idea where it came from. It says something about planning before doing, I think, which is what we've been doing with this fat-trimming exercise isn't it? And I think the words on the poster are plan, do, check and act."

"I believe 'Plan, Do, Check, Adjust' is another version of essentially the same thing," said Charlie. "And yes, it is about planning before doing, as we've been doing. But it goes beyond that with the 'check' and 'adjust' steps."

Charlie went on to explain PDCA in terms of the way his doctor was working with him on his health program: the *plan* the doctor had put together, the action's (*do*) he – Charlie – was taking as a result of that plan, the measurements (*check*) the doctor was taking on a regular basis and the way he would *adjust* Charlie's plan based on those measurements.

"That sounds sort of like what we're doing with our hand-packing line," said Yu. "We're making small adjustments as we go to try and hit the target we set ourselves."

"Or what my guys do when they're setting up a machine," said Jerry. "They run it for a few minutes, check the weight of the product coming off, make an adjustment to suit, then repeat the cycle until they get it right."

"You're both right," said Charlie. "As you can see, PDCA is just common sense in many ways. The challenge we have as a group is that we need to apply PDCA to the whole plant at once, with all the different plans that each area has. That's where our Fat Trimming Project Board comes in: it will help us manage the Plan – Do – Check – Adjust cycle while keeping us focused on the main goal, our 20 per cent cost reduction."

Charlie turned to the blank whiteboard behind him and drew a diagram.

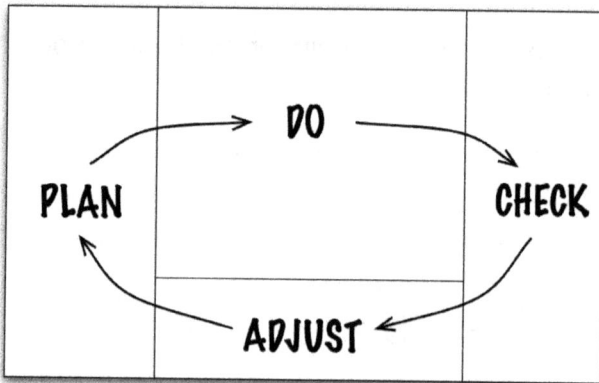

"This is an overview of the large board on the wall," said Charlie. "You'll notice that the large board is divided into four main sections, laid out as in this sketch. Each of those sections represents one of the four PDCA steps."

Charlie asked everyone to stand up and gather around the main board.

"This left-hand column is the 'Plan' section. At the top of the column is a table that summarizes the factory-wide plan — in essence that 20 per cent cut. Now, normally it would be the responsibility of each of you to summarize your own plan underneath that: your own contribution to meeting that 20 per cent target. To get things started I've done that for you this first time, so you can see that in this column we can get an overview of the 'total' plan."

"What's good about that is that we can really see how what we're doing fits into the overall picture," said Yu.

"Exactly," said Charlie. "How often in the past have we made change that seemed to make sense on one level but that we couldn't really understand the relevance of on a company scale. Now the whole picture is laid out for you."

Charlie moved to the 'Do' section of the board.

	This week					Next week					5 week plan				
DO															
	M	T	W	T	F	M	T	W	T	F	1	2	3	4	5
Charlie															
Martin															
Yu															

"This is the real working part of the board. As you can see, there is a row allocated to each of you. The rows are divided into sections for 'This week', 'Next week' and a 'Five week plan' and there are pockets in which you can place these cards." Charlie held up a plain card about the size of a normal index card.

"The idea is that each of you will use this section on pretty much a daily basis. You'll place cards into the pockets that outline actions your section is planning to take on a given day, or in the next five weeks. Most of those actions need to contribute to the plan — that's the critical link between 'Do' and 'Plan' on this board. There are different colored cards for other categories of action — for instance, red cards signify unplanned tasks like dealing with a breakdown or quality issue."

"Can I interrupt you there, Charlie," said Jerry. "This is starting to look like a lot of work — how much time are we going to spend keeping all these cards up to date?"

"Well, that depends," said Charlie. "Do you create some sort of to-do list for yourself at the moment?"

"Sometimes. But quite often I'm so busy that I don't get that far. Things just keep coming at me and I deal with them as they arrive."

"Which is exactly why something like this is important," said Charlie. "In a job like yours, or mine, or any leadership role really, it's very easy to keep busy by spending all your time reacting. But working that way almost guarantees that you'll never get around to the *important* tasks — the tasks that will help us meet our 20 per cent goal. Using a good planning tool like this board will help us all remember those important tasks."

"I already keep lists," said Martin, "but would prefer that I was able to keep them to myself. To me this is going to be doubling up — creating my own list and maintaining another list here."

"I'm with you on that Martin," said Charlie, "up to a point. I also have been in the habit of creating lists, but again, those lists often got to the point of being full of 'busy' stuff and devoid of 'important' stuff. On top of that, as your manager, I have to agree that I have some trepidation about sharing what I'm up to. I mean, you might work out that I don't do very much at all!" That brought a chuckle from the room.

"But it is well known that 'going public' creates a much greater likelihood that things will get done than keeping them to ourselves. It's true of my health situation – which is one of the reasons I'm being quite open about that. And it's true of work like ours. We have to look at this goal as a team goal, and work as a team to pull it off. To do that, we have to be open with each other. That doesn't mean that if a task allocated to Monday isn't achieved you'll be shot down in flames. This board is not about blame. It does mean that if you're struggling to get something done, someone else might be able to chip in and help you achieve it – say by attending a meeting on your behalf or supervising your line for a few hours, or whatever.

"Also, this board is here to record and track tasks that contribute to our plan – the white cards – or get in the way of meeting the plan – the red cards. You don't need to put on the board all the routine day-to-day operational stuff that you do to keep the plant running."

Jerry, Martin and a few others still didn't look convinced, but Charlie decided to press on. Anna had told him that many people felt the way they did when her company's board went up, but that most had come around to seeing the positives quite quickly once it was being used.

"As I said, this 'Do' section of the board will be your main working part. The idea would be that you each keep your own row up to date. It should be current each morning when you have your daily planning meeting. Then on Friday afternoons, in preparation for the following week, we meet together and shift everything forward. We'll obviously have to work out some details to make this work for us, but they'll best be worked out as we start to use it."

Moving to the right side of the board, Charlie said, "This section represents the 'Check' step of our PDCA cycle."

"We haven't talked a lot about measurements yet, but in summary, this section will contain a number of charts that show how well we're going against various targets. The main target, of course, is the 20 per cent cost reduction and so we will include a chart that shows the total value of cost savings identified and the total value of cost savings actually realized. Other charts will go into lower levels of detail by department – they need to reflect, as closely as possible, the plans on the opposite side of the board. One thing to say about this 'Check' section: we'll use graphs as much as possible to keep the whole thing visual and easy to understand at a glance. Each chart needs to be understandable by all of us, not just the team leader who is maintaining it."

"So we each look after our own chart or charts?" said Yu.

"We'll come up with some templates to make it easier, but yes – keeping the charts up to date will be your job."

"More work," grumbled Martin.

"Or a good opportunity for delegation," said Charlie. "All you need to do is find someone in your team – there's bound to be one amongst the younger members of the group at least – someone who likes computers and spreadsheets. It will be a good way to take advantage of their interest and get them involved. They can update the charts manually – you know, with an old fashioned pen – every day, then update and print a new version from the computer, say, weekly."

Charlie pointed to the bottom of the board.

"Along the bottom is our 'Adjust' section. Here is where we will record any changes to our original plans, for instance where our measurements have suggested there should be a change because targets aren't being met. We will also capture information about changes that we've made successfully and that will be 'locked in' for the time being. That information will include changes needed to documentation: procedures documents, user manuals and the like.

"So there you have it. We have a bit of work to do before it is complete, but our 'PDCA Board' is ready to go in the meantime. What I'd like you all to do is go through the report and plans you were going to share with us today and translate those onto cards that can be applied to the 'this week', 'next week' or 'five weeks' part of the board. The main things to remember are one task per card, and use white cards for work that contributes to our project and red cards for unplanned tasks – that is, tasks relating to unplanned or unforeseen circumstances that get in the way of our plans. And you don't need to create cards for all the various routine and operational tasks that you do every day."

After answering a few questions, Charlie felt a bit like a school teacher giving his class an exercise as the team worked silently for the next few minutes. When they all had a few cards done he asked them to place their cards onto the board in line with the times by which they would have the task done, describing their plans to the group as they went.

As usual, some of the team took to the task with great enthusiasm while others were a bit reticent. Martin, in particular, seemed to be holding back. When he came up to the board he placed a couple of cards on to it, but no more.

"I'm just finding it really hard to make commitments I don't think I can keep," he said. "There's still a bit of work to do sorting out this underweight product problem."

Charlie tried to reassure him. "That's fine, Martin. What you need to do is make sure you include those tasks on the board – as red cards – and also include some of your other tasks, but push them out to the following week or even beyond that. It's only by everyone seeing what you're up against that we'll be able to help. Remember – it's in the interests of all of us to meet our main goal, so as I've said before, this has to be a team effort."

Martin shrugged and wrote out four red cards, which he allocated to the first three days of the next week. He then wrote out two more white cards, which he placed against 'Week 4'. One of those cards, he explained, was running a training session for his team on the 'learning to see' concept, which he felt they hadn't really understood the first time around.

"Why don't I do that for you," said Yu. "It might help if they heard it from someone else, and I could bring one of my operators, Tony, who has really mastered it. It would be even better for them to hear it from another operator. We could do that next Thursday."

Martin hesitated, but when he looked at Charlie he seemed to remember the 'team' message before Charlie had a chance to restate it. "Okay Yu. That would be great. Thanks." He reallocated the card to the next Thursday while Yu made a note in her diary.

Charlie was about to wrap up the meeting when Yu asked another question.

"I can see how this board will be great for all of us to keep track of progress, but I'm wondering if we can do something similar on the floor. I think it's important that our leading hands and operators can see what progress we're making against our own goals, and also what we're contributing to the main goal."

"I see what you mean," said Charlie. "I guess there's no reason why we couldn't have local versions of this board in each department — boards that focus on the plans, actions and so on for that department. All you'd need is your own plan on the left-hand side, and your own measures on the right — plus perhaps the overall plan and overall goal-tracking chart. What do you all think?"

"So it's like a cascade," said Jerry, "with information flowing back and forth from the local boards to this main board?"

"Exactly," said Charlie.

With general agreement on this idea, Charlie took a card from the pile of blanks and wrote on it. As he placed it onto the board against the next Friday, he said, "Jerry, I might need the help of one of your fitters to install these, but I'll organize all the components by the time we meet next week."

As his team packed up to leave, Charlie added, "I would encourage all of you to bring your teams up and show them this board — especially when you are trying to explain the local one. They need to see their own board in context."

After everyone had left the room, Charlie stood back and had a long look at his PDCA Board. Not bad, he thought. With cards in the 'Do' section, it was really starting to take shape. He looked down at his generous stomach. Perhaps, he thought, I should put one of these up in the kitchen at home as well.

⁂

The next day, Saturday, was clear and mild. Charlie rang Jason and suggested a ride on their bikes. His friend was on the doorstep within minutes and the two men took to the road.

As they trundled along, Charlie described his week to Jason. "We've only just started with this board, but already I can feel how powerful a tool it could be. Never before have I been able to describe such clear links between the company's overall goals and what the folks on the floor are doing. And I'm a manager! Heaven knows how detached everyone on the floor has felt. The strange thing is — and this seems so obvious in hindsight — that I don't think we've ever given this any proper thought in the past. We just assume that we can name a goal, like our cost-reduction target, and expect everyone to implicitly understand how their own actions can contribute to that goal."

"It's just the same in my world," said Jason. "The bank has lots of big goals, and we have all sorts of meetings and workshops to try and communicate those goals to the staff, but I don't think we communicate that link very well at all. When you're one of tens of thousands of employees, it can be pretty hard to see how your own actions can make a difference to the whole."

They turned left onto a boulevard that followed the winding course of a river, joining a large number of other cyclists sharing the same route.

"It's strange, you know," said Jason. "You wouldn't think there was much in common between your chocolate making and my bank. But the more you describe what you're doing, the more I realize how many similarities there are. It's all just processes, isn't it — yours are just potentially a whole lot messier."

"Very true," said Charlie. "And I guess you don't tend to have problems of underweight product at the bank."

The boulevard ended with a gentle but lengthy climb, and as the two men arrived at the base of the rise a stiff breeze hit their faces. They slowed to a crawl, Charlie's breath getting heavier as they crept upwards. When they finally reached the top of the hill, Charlie signaled to Jason that he needed to stop. He climbed off his bike and sat heavily on the curb.

"Are you okay, mate?" said Jason.

"I will be ... just give me a minute ..." said Charlie. He slumped a bit further and said, "Feeling ... faint."

Jason pulled his mobile phone out of his pocket and dialed. "I need an ambulance," he said.

5 Check

Charlie's doctor read from his computer screen for a few minutes then turned to Charlie.

"What happened to you on Saturday was more a warning sign than a health problem," said the doctor. "The cardiologist in the emergency room checked all your vital signs and found nothing of any consequence. That's why she discharged you pretty much straight away. Nevertheless, your body's response to that extra pressure you put it under is a signal that perhaps you pushed yourself too far. Now, how's your weight going?"

"I'm down a couple of kilos according to my measurements."

The doctor nodded. He asked Charlie to step up on the scales to double check his weight, then measured his blood pressure as well.

"I wouldn't want that fainting spell a couple of days ago to put you off," said the doctor. "My measurements indicate that you have turned the corner and you are making progress. Your weight has come down a little – my scales show you've lost one and a half kilograms so far. And your blood pressure is down a little as well. These are what we would expect from the plan that I put together for you, so it seems that you are sticking to that. What you need to do now is continue to stick to that plan ... which does not include cycling up long hills into strong head winds. There will be time for that, but not until you've lost a bit more weight and built up a bit more aerobic fitness."

Charlie smiled. "As you've said many times before, we have a *plan*, and my job is to stick to it – to *do* what we've planned and nothing else," he said.

"You got it," said the doctor. "In a few weeks I'll send you back to the cardiologist for an ECG, which will act as a *check* and give us a more detailed picture of how your heart is responding to the plan, and we can reassess and *adjust* the plan after that. But in the meantime: stick to our plan. Having said that, I'd like you to have a few days off to give your body a rest – preferably the week if you can manage that."

"That's tough, Doc. It's not a great time to be away." Charlie thought for a moment. "Tell you what. I'll stay at home until Thursday – I'll do what I can by phone and email. But there's a meeting I really would like to get to on Friday, so perhaps I could go back in then. How does that sound?"

When Anna arrived home that evening with Jack and Sophie in tow, Charlie was hunched over his laptop.

"I thought you were supposed to be resting," she said. "Working from home isn't resting."

"I know," said Charlie. "But having got our PDCA Board up I really want to maintain some momentum. And I did commit to organizing the small boards I told you about this week."

Anna pulled a chair up and sat down beside Charlie.

"Don't forget that the whole point of these strategy deployment boards, or whatever you want to call yours, is to share the load. Your staff are quite capable. Why don't you just see how they go with the board this week. If they get off track you can correct things next week, but you might be surprised. In the meantime, just take care of yourself."

Charlie put his hand on Anna's shoulder. "You're right, of course. I'll just send off an email to my team to explain my situation and ask them to hold the fort. I've already arranged for the small-board components to be purchased. After that, I'll take it easy. Okay?"

"Okay," said Anna with a nod.

* * *

On getting into the factory the following Friday, Charlie went straight to the meeting room to have a look at the project board. He felt like a child on Christmas morning, wondering what surprises were waiting for him. He knew his team were perfectly capable of continuing without him normally, but he wanted to see whether they had started using the board without prompting.

As soon as he walked into the meeting room, a first glance at the board gave him his answer. Some of the team were actively using the board. Cards from days earlier in the week had either been removed (presumably because the tasks on those cards had been completed) or they had been moved forward. Others – Martin stood out here – looked as though they had not used the board at all. Martin's red cards – placed the previous Friday – hadn't been moved, and he didn't seem to have added any white cards either. Charlie looked at Jerry's row and was pleased to see he had made some attempt to get his plan up to date, though he had nothing planned beyond the next week.

Charlie went over to the board and updated his own row, moving his cards for this week forward. He also removed one card that had been assigned to Friday. Then he walked to his office to see what had piled up in his in-tray while he'd been away.

A couple of hours later, Charlie's team started to arrive for their meeting. On the hour, Charlie was surprised that the only person missing was Yu. No one knew where she was. He hesitated — he didn't want to break his 'start on time' rule but equally was concerned that Yu probably had a good reason for not being there and not having let him know that she wouldn't be. Acutely aware of not wanting to show favoritism, Charlie opted to start the meeting.

As he opened his mouth to speak, Greta from Yu's area appeared at the door.

"Yu asked me to sit in for her for a little while, if that's okay. She's with Samantha — a new girl — who has just received some bad news about a family member. They're waiting for her husband to pick her up."

"Of course, Greta. Please come in."

Charlie began the meeting by sharing some company

results from the recently closed-off month. "As we've been fearing, sales are flat," he said. "They have been for four months now and there is little sign of any potential change in the short term."

"People are generally hesitant about spending money at the moment, aren't they?" asked Martin. "I know my family is, because my wife's job looks very shaky. It's just all a bit uncertain out there. Couldn't that be contributing to these figures?"

"Unfortunately it is not so simple," said Charlie. "We get detailed sales data from the supermarket chains and those figures show that while our sales are stable, a couple of the imported brands, which have dropped their prices recently, are increasing their market shares. Obviously this is not a good thing, but it gets potentially worse when, as the sales team are telling me, the supermarkets are starting to make noises about shelf-space: if we can't justify our prominent position on their shelves, they will give more space to these imports. And that will only make matters worse."

"So what's the plan?" asked Jerry.

"Well none of this is really news to Antonio and the directors, so the plan remains unchanged: reduce costs. Reducing costs will give the business options. The potential to cut prices without sacrificing profit margin or, more likely, to tweak our range to provide more value to customers – you know, the old '10 per cent more for no extra cost' promotion for example."

"So why aren't we doing that now?"

"Well basically the directors are happy with our 'fat trimming' plans, as I've told you, but they want to see some results on the board before they start giving chocolate away. They're not expecting the full 20 per cent cost reduction overnight, but they do want to see real progress."

Charlie moved across to the project board.

"You'll notice that I've added a chart to the 'Check' section on the project board this morning. The overall summary chart shows our costs and productivity were essentially unchanged last month from the previous month. Now, I think we're doing better than that, but as you know there is always a bit of lag in these figures. It takes a while before a change we make down on the floor actually shows up in the books. That's why we still need to add some other charts here that will show more local results associated with the projects in each of your departments, hopefully with less lag."

Greta raised her hand and Charlie invited her to speak. "I don't know if this is the right time to bring this up – I can't say I'm understanding everything you're talking about – but Yu did give me this chart that shows progress on our main project area."

Charlie took the graph from Greta and looked it over. "Excellent," he said. "Greta, you understand more than you think." Greta smiled and straightened in her chair, holding her head a little higher.

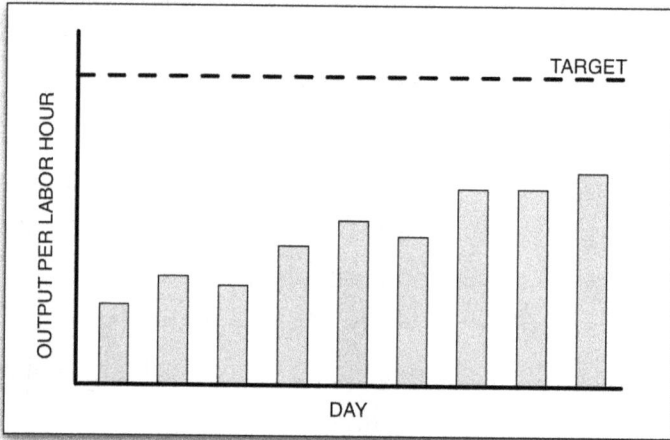

Passing the printout around the room, Charlie said, "This chart shows output from the hand-packing area against direct labor hours on a daily basis over the last two weeks. It's not a direct cost measure, but it is relevant because labor reorganization is Yu's main sub-project – the one where she expects to make her biggest savings. Notice the red line: that's the area's target for this chart.

"Still looks a fair way off," said Martin.

"It does," said Charlie. "But that's not really the point at this early stage. The point is that it's moving in the right direction because of the creative efforts of people like Greta. The good thing about the chart is that it shows Greta and her co-workers that their efforts are paying off. If you look at the board in Yu's row, you can see that they have various other initiatives planned that will probably push this chart closer to their goal."

"That's right," said Greta. "Next week we're going to try a different arrangement for the wrapped candy assortment. We think we can make some quite good changes there."

Charlie added the chart to the board. "If we can put one chart here from each area that shows progress on that area's main project, plus the overall chart, we'll have a good picture of what's going on."

Charlie stood back from the board. "Now, hopefully, you start to see the way our PDCA Board works." He pointed out how Yu's plan, on the left-hand side, included labor efficiency as a goal. In the 'Do' section of the board were the actions they were taking — and when they would take them – to implement that part of the plan. And now, with this chart, the 'Check' part was also being included.

"The way this is progressing, the team may not need to adjust their plan very much. But what will eventually go into the 'Adjust' area of the board are the new, finalized layouts and labor assignments for the area. That would round off the whole picture … until they start the process again."

"Now, let's look at what's been going on in each of your areas, using the board as a reference," said Charlie. "Jerry?"

"Okay. Well, our first goal has been to have a bit of a tidy-up in the workshop. We realize that we are spending a lot of time looking for things, and we are also wasting or overbuying quite a few consumable materials because they aren't put away properly and get lost. For instance, we found five bags of the same washer after the workbenches were cleared and tidied up. The thinking there is that we can cut consumable costs to some degree if we make maximum use of what we already have and lose less."

"Makes a lot of sense, Jerry," said Charlie. "Any thoughts about how you might measure improvement there and show it in our 'Check' section?"

"We'll create a chart showing consumable spend by month – that's pretty easy to do. It will go up and down a bit, depending on what happens in the factory, but we think we can get it trending down."

"Great. Now, I notice that you have one card still allocated to this Wednesday," said Charlie.

"Yes. That was to pull apart the Number 1 wrapping machine, which is producing a lot of wastage. Unfortunately we couldn't get on to it due to production constraints."

"That would be because Jerry didn't talk to me before putting the card on the board," said Martin.

"Well I did talk to the planners. It seems they were unaware that you were planning overtime," said Jerry. "And if you'd come to the morning planning meeting on Wednesday perhaps you could have told me then."

"If the machine wasn't generating so much waste we wouldn't have had to run overtime, and I would have been at the meeting."

"Gentlemen, stop right there. We've had this conversation before, many times," said Charlie. "But it raises a couple of important points about how we use this board. First, one reason the board is so visible is so we can share information and see what each other is planning – not so we can fight about it, but so we can work together to make things happen. But, Martin, that won't work unless you turn up at the planning meeting each morning and review the board together.

"The second point is that if something doesn't get done on its scheduled day – for whatever reason – it needs to be rescheduled. Nothing should be left behind on the board. You'll notice that I've moved most of my own cards forward on the board as a result of being away this week. The exception is the components for the smaller boards for the factory floor. Jerry, if you send one of your fitters down to the inwards warehouse they'll find all those waiting for them.

"Martin, I notice that you haven't moved any of your cards at all."

Martin looked directly at Charlie. "I'm sorry, Charlie, but it's been flat out. To be honest, I think getting the work done is more important than playing with these cards."

"I'm sorry Martin, but I think you've got the wrong idea about this," said Yu, who had walked into the room as Martin was speaking. "Those of us who have been spending five minutes – and it is just five minutes – with the board each morning have been moving our plans along. I'm sorry to be blunt, but you haven't. You're stuck in this reaction mode where everything you do is, well, a red card. It's not that we don't all have unplanned issues crop up. Of course we do.

We just don't let those things get in the way of making the more important changes — with the help of our teams." Yu gestured towards Greta.

Martin, looking somewhat chastened, nodded. "Perhaps I could get Tim to help with updating the PDCA Board. He's been doing most of the work on our board downstairs."

"Perfect," said Charlie. "And I'm sure Yu or even Greta would be happy to help if he needs any guidance."

Speaking to the whole team, Charlie said, "I want you to all learn from this situation. This wrapping machine needs repair because it is wasting both product and time — and therefore generating all sorts of unnecessary costs. At the moment, rather than investing the time to have it repaired, it is simply being run longer and harder, which is only exacerbating the waste situation. This is unsustainable. So — Jerry and Martin — you need to work this out together, with the planners, and update the board to match that plan."

Jerry said, "Sounds good to me. In addition, you'll notice that another of my cards is the development of a detailed preventative maintenance plan. Martin has said in the past that we've let this slip, and he's right. We intend to get this back on track so that our maintenance becomes proactive instead of reactive — white cards instead of red, if you like. That will reduce our costs in the medium term, particularly in terms of overtime."

"And will you measure that too?" asked Charlie.

"Yes, we'll track both the number of machines maintained, and the hours spent on breakdowns," said Jerry.

By the end of the meeting Charlie was feeling confident that the overall direction of his team and their use of the PDCA Board were on track. There were details to be ironed out, but there was no doubt that the board had already created more open communication – if not always as civil as he would have liked. Charlie was most pleased with the extent to which his team were starting to bounce ideas off each other, adapting successful initiatives from one area into others. It was as if the good ideas were starting to snowball.

. . .

As the weeks passed, the team started to settle into a pattern. The project board became an integral part of the team leaders' morning planning meeting, the leaders using that meeting to update their row on the PDCA Board while also updating their colleagues on progress. Every Friday morning Charlie would hold his weekly meeting at which the team as a whole would review any new progress updates in the 'Check' section and plan the following week. Every month, the entire PDCA Board was reviewed and updated, paying particular attention to the charts.

Down on the factory floor a smaller board was installed in each department. These showed the overall company plan and the local department plan, but not the plans of all the other departments. They also showed the company and department 'scorecards': charts showing progress against the various targets.

Charlie noticed how having a strong system like this created a sort of rhythm to his work and that of his team – a rhythm that had certainly not been there in the past. Yes, things continued to go wrong, but these unexpected events no longer diverted all attention away from the main goal. Overall, it was noticeably reducing the amount of stress that he was building up over a week.

Even Martin, who had been so resistant in those first few weeks, started to see the benefits of this after a while. And as someone who had always had trouble translating company plans into a way that his operators could under-stand, Martin found the strong links between the main PDCA Board and the local department board very helpful. As

Charlie walked the floor he noticed how Martin was starting to be a more effective leader by shifting his point of view between the 'big picture' and the detail (where previously he had tended to get stuck in the detail).

* * *

Later Charlie was taking a walk around the factory floor when Yu called out to him and waved for him to join her. She was having a team meeting and wanted Charlie to listen to what they were discussing.

"We've been talking about our board," she said. "Everyone appreciates keeping in touch with what's going on, and we like being able to show others what we've been doing too. Previously when we thought we were doing well we often didn't think we were given any credit for our efforts. Now we can use the board to demand bragging rights."

Yu's team nodded as one.

"But there's a feeling that we could do better." She looked at her operator, Samantha.

"I used to work in another factory where we made parts for cars," said Samantha. "One of the things they did there was use a lot of pictures and lights and symbols, as well as really simple scoreboards, so that everyone could understand how things were going at a glance. Our boards are great, but they don't give us that sort of 'at a glance' update – you really have to stop and read the charts to know whether we're doing well or not."

"Samantha was telling me that the other thing about these more visual 'signs'," added Yu, "is that they give more timely information. The charts on our boards get updated once every couple of weeks. Of course we also measure our daily performance but that doesn't go on there. And even daily performance as a whole doesn't allow us to make changes during the day if things are getting out of whack."

"I see what you mean," said Charlie. "Sounds like you're talking about having something closer to a car speedometer – something that gives instant feedback. So, Samantha, what sorts of things did this factory have along these lines?"

Samantha went on to describe a number of different visual feedback tools, including:

- Simple scoreboards on each manufacturing production line – just ruled-up whiteboards – on which output was updated against target by the hour. If the team on any line could see output dipping, they could take quick action to work out why, and make corrections, rather than allowing the poor productivity to continue all day.

- Even simpler symbols to show progress as it happened. "We used traffic light symbols − red, yellow and green − to show output against target. And we used simple faces − sad, neutral and happy − to indicate quality and reject levels. Every department used the same system so that anyone walking around the plant could quickly gauge how the place was going."

- Lights, called 'Andon' lights, attached to each machine. "The lights are green when the machine is running well, but automatically turn orange or red when the machine detects some sort of fault or stops. These were amazing, because when a light went red − accompanied by a horn sound − you would immediately, without anyone making a phone call, see people coming from all directions − operators, technicians and managers − towards the troublesome machine.

"Apart from all these symbols that showed our progress, the factory and the offices used lots of visual ways to help keep things tidy. In the factory they had marked up the floor with colored tape to show where, say, a rubbish bin should be, or a mop and bucket. All our tools were stored on boards with a sort of shadow or silhouette behind the tool so you knew where to put it back. In the offices they even had a tape mark running diagonally across the spines of binders in a group so it was easy to keep them in the correct order."

Charlie looked at Yu. "This all sounds quite useful. Do you think it would help us with cost reduction, though, given that is our main focus at the moment?"

"Yes, certainly," said Yu. "We even did a test. The other day we asked everyone to keep track of how much time they spent looking for a tool, or anything else like a mop and bucket. We used stopwatches to do the timing. In one day, the total time spent looking for things was 25 minutes. We repeated the test the next day and it was 35 minutes. Let's say half an hour a day over a month: that's over 10 hours of time spent looking for things. It really adds up.

"We also recorded how much time we needed to wait for someone to come and look at a faulty machine," said Greta. "Over a week we lost nearly three hours in total doing that – and that's just the waiting time, not the lost production.

"Saving this time might not necessarily allow us to

reduce the labor needed on any one line," said Yu, "but it could certainly help reduce our overtime – and that's one of our mini-projects."

"I'm impressed," said Charlie. "I'm not sure we could get something as fancy as those Andon lights installed in the short term, but most of the other things you mentioned, well, you should be able to do those quite easily don't you think?"

"Definitely," said Yu. "We didn't think the lights and horns were going to be able to happen very soon either, but someone suggested a really simple solution in the interim. If we tie brightly colored ribbons to the cooling fan outlets on the machines, those ribbons will be streaming all the time when the machine is running, but will stop streaming and fall when the machine stops."

"That's a very clever idea," said Charlie. "The good thing about it is that Peter and I would be able to see the ribbons from our offices when they are flying. That would be a good way to draw attention to an issue."

Yu laughed. "I thought of that too."

Charlie drew Yu aside after the meeting broke up. "I just wanted to say what a great job you are doing, Yu. I get the impression that maybe working in this chocolate factory is becoming fun for you again."

"Yes, it is," said Yu. "I said to you a few weeks ago that I thought we were lacking purpose — now we have more than enough."

"I'm very pleased," said Charlie. "Keep up the great work."

Charlie's phone rang. He showed the screen to Yu. "Looks like the boss wants me. I'll see you later."

* * *

Peter stood up as Charlie knocked on the open door and entered his office. "We have an issue that could be quite big."

"What is it, Peter?"

"I've just had a call from the Weights and Measures section of Consumer Affairs. Seems a number of under-weight products have found their way onto the market. I don't have many details at the moment — not even which products are involved and whether it's related to the bar line issue of a little while ago. Anyway, Weights and Measures have been under political pressure lately after a few well pub-licized stuff ups. They could do with a good news story and, to them, 'outing' a big company like us would be just that."

"Does that mean they intend going to the media? That

would be catastrophic to our reputation – it would sure give our competitors a boost."

"They've said they won't go to the media just yet, but they have no choice but to come down heavily on us."

"Which means?"

"They'll be doing a full – and I mean full – inspection. A team of inspectors are going to visit us in a week. They'll go over the place with a fine-toothed comb and then write a hefty report. They'll want to know exactly what systems are in place to prevent underweight product, and they'll want to see all those systems in action. If they find anything significantly out of place, anything which suggests to them that there is a good chance of finding more out-of-specification product out there, they'll have no choice but to shut us down while we get things back in order. At that point they'd have to go public too."

"Wow," said Charlie. "A shut down for just a couple of days would wipe away most of the savings we've made so far."

"That's right. So it can't happen. At the same time you and your team need to keep an eye on the main game. We can't let this jeopardize progress on the cost-cutting project."

All of a sudden Charlie's heart started pounding.

6   Adjust

"How are you feeling?" said the doctor as he removed the cuff of the blood pressure meter from Charlie's arm.

"I've been pretty good, Doc. Much more in control at work – at least I was until yesterday. I'm feeling healthier too. I've lost five kilograms, which I think is a little behind target. I do know that I can get up a flight of stairs at work now without feeling out of breath at the top."

"Well, that's a positive. Your cardiology reports are certainly improved – the last ECG showed some improvement in the overall health of your heart. Your blood pressure has come down a bit, but it's still not quite at a healthy level. As for weight loss, five kilograms in four months is okay, but I would like to see it coming off a little quicker.

You're still a way off being in safe territory."

The doctor looked over Charlie's charts again.

"Let's summarize where we are," said the doctor. "We made a *plan* four months ago. Apart from a couple of deviations, you've been *doing* what we planned. Now our *checks* show that your heart health has improved but your weight is still higher than it should be. We can now *adjust* the plan to try and address that. I think it's time to do that by changing your fitness program a bit. Over time the body tends to get used to a given fitness regime and the effects slow. What we might do now is alter your cardio exercise regime to take advantage of the fact that your heart health has improved. That, in turn, should see the weight start to come off a little more quickly. What do you think about doing some work in a gym or fitness center?"

"Time will be a challenge, but if it has to be done I'll find a way," said Charlie.

"I think now would be a good time," said the doctor. "This is a phase when a lot of people go backwards. They see some progress and think they can relax – that the danger has passed. We're a long way away from there. The gym will give you a new challenge. And we will continue our cycle of regular visits to check your progress and adjust the plan to suit."

. . .

The next day Charlie, working in his office, looked out of his window overlooking the factory floor. In Yu's area he could see a number of green streamers fluttering from various machines. Talk about doers, he thought. Below him, he noticed Jerry and Martin engaged in animated conversation. Charlie frowned. As a father, he preferred not to intervene in his children's fights, rather letting them learn by sorting things out themselves. These two, though, were a different story: two 50-something men who seemed like they would never learn. He sighed, stood up and headed towards the stairs.

Jerry and Martin were talking with raised voices when Charlie arrived. "What's going on?" he said.

"It's this underweight issue," said Martin. "We've managed to track down a likely culprit. Only now does Jerry tell me that he found a calibration issue with a number of the automated check-weighers a month ago."

Charlie looked at Jerry. "That's true, but we thought we had it under control," said Jerry. "The problem is fixed now, and it would never have led to underweight product if the nozzles on the enrobers had been properly monitored and cleaned every few hours. We asked Tim to put an extra person on this task but he was overruled by Martin, who was concerned about the extra cost reflecting on his department."

"Well perhaps if someone had told me the full story."

"Okay, okay," said Charlie. "This is all very nice, but we're not looking for blame here. What we're trying to do is stop underweight product getting out to the stores with poor service to our customers, and it sounds like both of you have identified holes in our system that need to be plugged. What we need to do now is revisit those systems, make sure they're working as they should be and that the chances of this happening again are minimal. If we do all that, the inspectors will be happy − and so will our customers. Before next week I need both of you to make sure that all these systems − from checking calibrations to cleaning nozzles to informing each other of what's going on − are in place and tightened up. Alright?"

Martin and Jerry nodded. "Fair enough," said Martin. "I think we're actually doing that."

"Good. That was the impression I got when I looked at the project board briefly a bit earlier. You both seemed to have a number of red cards in place and most of them are related to underweight product risk by the look of them."

"Correct," said Jerry. "We've done an audit of the systems that are already in place to prevent underweight product – you'll remember we talked about that on Friday. The cards on the board relate to some actions as a result of that audit."

"So why the disagreement this morning?" asked Charlie.

"I only learned about the calibration issue this morning," said Martin. "It came up during a discussion about checkweighing procedures at the planning meeting. I think things like that could embarrass us in front of the inspectors."

"Well, yes, but let's remember that despite its importance, the inspection is secondary here. Making product within specification is mostly about giving our customers what they are paying for. So let's not lose sight of the big picture, while recognizing that our systems do have to be spick and span by the time the inspectors arrive. Could we go up and have a look at the plan?" said Charlie.

At the board, Jerry and Martin walked Charlie through the various 'red card' unplanned actions that they were taking to refine the weight-control systems before the Weights and Measures inspectors' visit in a few days time.

* * *

"I'm impressed," said Charlie. "I'm impressed by the way you're using the board and I'm impressed by the methodical approach you're both taking. Did you notice how you've taken the same 'Plan – Do – Check – Adjust' approach to these small unplanned projects that we're taking overall?"

Jerry and Martin looked at each other. "Not really," said Jerry. "I just thought what we were doing was common sense – the same as we do when we're maintaining a machine: work out what needs doing, do the job, check that it's working as expected and adjust as necessary."

"You're right. PDCA is largely common sense – but as I've said before, common sense isn't always so common. Now, while we're here. Last week we didn't have a lot of time to look at your 'fat trimming' project work. Could you run me through that briefly please."

Jerry pointed to a chart in the 'Check' section of the board. "This is our major focus at the moment," he said. "We're aiming to get the product changeover time on the chocolate bar lines down to an average of 45 minutes. When we started measuring it, the average was closer to 80 minutes. Aside from giving me 35 more minutes of two fitters' time for every change, Martin and I worked out that he could remove one overtime shift a week if we can achieve that."

"That would be a cost saving of nearly 5 per cent on my line alone, plus whatever Jerry saves," said Martin.

"The chart shows that we've got the average down to about 55 minutes, but it has leveled off in the last three weeks or so. Now, as you can see in this adjustment plan…" Jerry pointed to a document in the 'Adjust' section of the board "and these two cards on mine and Martin's rows, we plan next week to make some further changes that will hopefully pull that changeover time down further still."

"My card relates to some cleaning issues that slow down how quickly Jerry's guys can get on to the machine at the end of a run. We have some ideas there which we'll implement …" Martin looked at the board "next Wednesday."

The three of them chatted through some other initiatives for a few minutes. They were about to disperse when a young staff member entered the room.

"Moira," said Charlie, "is that an update for us?"

"Yes," said Moira. "Total cost savings in place to date, by department." She handed the chart to Charlie.

"Look at that," said Charlie, replacing the previous chart

on the project board. "Four months in and we've dropped 7 per cent. Repeat that three times and we'll hit 21 per cent in 12 months, though it's likely it will be harder to reduce costs later in the year than now, when all the 'easy' savings are being made. Nevertheless, we are trimming fat more quickly from the factory than I am trimming it from myself." Charlie patted his belly with both hands. "I'll have to get a move on."

Jerry and Martin laughed, while Moira looked a little embarrassed. "Sorry, Moira. You don't need to know the gruesome details of my weight-loss program. Thank you for this chart."

"We might be going in the right direction," Jerry said to Martin, "but Yu's the star here. Look at that: she's taken 15 per cent off in her area already."

"Don't be hard on yourselves," said Charlie. "She's got a particularly enthusiastic team but, more to the point, her area is inherently more flexible than what you two are dealing with. And she's had less 'red card' issues to deal with too. The positive thing for me is that despite the red cards you've had to deal with, there is still some positive progress there. I'm confident you'll all get there in the end. You're doing well: keep up the good work."

As Jerry and Martin left the room, Charlie added, "And

stop with the bickering – okay?"

"Yes, boss," said Martin. He put an arm around Jerry's shoulders and said with a broad smile, "We love each other really!" Laughter accompanied them down the hall.

Passing the meeting room, Peter noticed Charlie in there and walked in.

"I was looking for you. There's been some sort of hold up in Weights and Measures, so they've had to delay their visit.

"Bureaucrats," mumbled Charlie.

Peter reported that the new date for the visit would be in six weeks time. The department promised a preliminary report two weeks after that: the same day that the directors were due to meet and review progress on the factory's cost-cutting measures. "Word is that if the directors aren't happy with progress they will ask Antonio to start obligatory layoffs very quickly. As a negative report from the inspectors would wipe away the savings you've made to date, it would in turn almost certainly lead to layoffs also. That Friday in eight weeks is going to be pretty important to the future of this plant."

◦ ◦ ◦

"So you've joined a gym," said Jason a couple of evenings later. "Walking with me every other night isn't doing it for you? Plus the weekend bike rides?"

"These walks are good, as are the bike rides," said Charlie, "but not enough, apparently. I need to trim the fat off more quickly."

"Ah, well. I'm sure you look terrific in a leotard."

"Very funny," said Charlie.

The friends walked for a while, chatting on various topics before the subject turned to work.

"Seems to me you are getting on top of things. From my point of view you are looking more relaxed," said Jason.

"Yes, there's no doubt. What's interesting to me is how much having everything laid out in front of us, on the project board, creates a feeling of being on top of it all. Even when something goes wrong, or comes at us unexpectedly, we just make adjustments to suit. When this inspection business first came up it seemed like a serious hassle, but after we stood back and looked at it in the context of everything else that's going on, it didn't seem that bad. In the past it was always about kneejerk reactions to things as they appeared on the road immediately in front of us. Now it is about looking well down the road and adjusting our driving to suit the conditions."

"You know the other thing that stands out for me," said Jason. "You always used to see all this stuff in terms of yourself: 'My issue is …', 'My problem is …', 'If only I could …' Now when you talk about these things the words you use are 'us' and 'we' and 'our'. It's not that you were egocentric before – far from it – but you did allow the bulk of the responsibility to rest on your shoulders. Sounds to me like you're now doing this with your team – you're no longer seeing your management as requiring that you take all of the pressure on yourself."

Charlie thought about that for a few minutes. "You're absolutely right, though I hadn't realized it until just now. Funny, isn't it. I didn't need to do a whole lot of team-building exercises; all I had to do was involve my team more and share the responsibilities and, like magic, they became more of a team."

They rounded a corner and found themselves at the base of a long flight of stairs.

"Still, while that's all good, we're not out of the woods yet," said Charlie. "In eight weeks time it could still fall around our feet if the directors aren't happy. Forced layoffs would be very hard to swallow, not only for me but for my whole team and everyone else. But it is going to be touch and go."

Charlie set off up the stairs and was surprised to find himself alone when he got to the top. Looking back down, there was Jason – breathlessly struggling to ascend the last dozen steps.

"Where … where did that come from?" said Jason. "You flew up those stairs."

"Must be a benefit of going to the gym," said Charlie with a grin.

7   Progress

"So, Daddy, what's happening at the chocolate factory today?" said Sophie through a mouthful of toast.

"Don't talk with your mouth full, Sophie. It's quite a big day for the chocolate factory, Sweetie. Some people are going to make some important decisions about the future," said Charlie.

"I hope they're good decisions. Daddy, for my party this year do you think you could take me and my friends on an excursion to the factory? I remember you took Jack once when he was littler."

Charlie looked at Anna. "Last week the Weights and Measures inspectors, now the kids," he smiled. Looking back at Sophie he said, "That sounds like a good idea, but I can't promise it yet

Sophie. Let me talk to some people and see what can be organized."

"Yippee!" said Sophie.

"Don't tell your friends yet, will you. I haven't said 'Yes' yet."

Sophie nodded seriously.

"So when will you have some answers today?" said Anna.

"The inspection report has been promised to us by midday. Then the directors meet from one o'clock. We really want the inspection to be all clear before the Board meeting so that that's behind us. Then the directors can focus on our cost-cutting efforts which, hopefully, are enough to keep them happy for the time being."

Charlie swallowed the last of his tea and stood up. "I'd better go. Antonio and Peter want a briefing this morning ahead of the rest of the day."

"Don't forget you're taking me to get my learner's permit tonight, Dad," said Jack.

"No problem, Jack. I'll be home by half past four."

Antonio and Charlie sat with Peter in his office.

"I've read the Board papers," said Antonio. "I'm impressed. The numbers you're presenting look very promising."

Charlie said, "How about we go for a walk around the plant, which would put those numbers into a fuller perspective. Then you can sit in on my team meeting and see our PDCA Board in action."

Antonio looked at his watch then down his front at his shiny shoes. "Is that really necessary?"

"I think you will look at things quite differently if you see them first hand. The numbers only tell you so much." Charlie smiled cheekily. "And I promise you won't dirty your shoes."

"Alright. But let's make it quick."

As the three of them walked around the factory, Charlie pointed out the many changes that had taken place over the preceding months.

"I have to say the place looks a lot tidier," said Antonio.

"Yes, one of the things most teams realized early on was how much time they were spending looking for things. So there was a big push on to clear out space and get organized. It has worked well. The best thing is that it has created an environment in which 'order' is the norm. If something is out of place now, it really looks out of place and gets dealt with quite quickly."

"And these green and yellow dots," said Antonio. "What do they mean?"

Charlie noticed Greta and waved to her to join them. "Greta, this is Antonio Smith, our CEO. Could you explain the traffic lights to him, please."

"Sure," said Greta. She guided Antonio over to her area and started showing him around.

"There's a lot of confidence there," said Peter. "Six months ago if you'd asked a leading hand to talk to the CEO, let alone show him around, they would have run a mile."

"Yes, it's amazing what giving people a bit of empowerment does," said Charlie. "And they do have a lot to show off."

Antonio rejoined them after a few minutes, noticeably enthused. "These folks have really taken to this task, haven't they? It's great to see."

At the bar line, Antonio asked Charlie to explain the local project board. Charlie showed him how the board outlined the plans for the area, and summarized the results so far.

"It will make more sense when we get upstairs and you can put it in context." Charlie looked at his watch. "And we need to head up there, as my meeting is due to start in a few minutes."

Antonio talked to Peter as they walked back towards the offices. As they came up the stairs, he turned to Charlie. "It seems that making the factory more lean is having a positive effect on you too. You're looking a lot healthier."

"Thanks Antonio," said Charlie. "I'm feeling a lot healthier too – and a lot more on top of my job."

"Well that certainly shows," said Antonio.

They entered the meeting room a couple of minutes before the meeting was due to start. Charlie introduced the CEO to a couple of his team who had not previously met him. Peter excused himself as he was expecting a call from Weights and Measures.

"Okay, everyone," said Charlie. "Let's see how our fat trimming is going."

One by one the team leaders took to the floor and updated the meeting on their area. For Antonio's benefit, Charlie had them summarize their original plans, describe the main actions that had been taken and that were planned for the future, show their results so far and the contribution to the overall target, and any adjustments to their plans or finalized changes.

Jerry explained a couple of red cards in his action plan, the result of an unexpected breakdown on one of the chocolate tanks. "Everything we do is on this Plan – Do – Check – Adjust cycle," he explained to Antonio. "Our whole fat trimming project follows that cycle, but so do smaller side projects like repairing this tank."

After Martin's turn, Antonio said, "So the charts you've just shown me for your area are the same ones that I saw down near the bar line. Is that correct?"

"Yes," said Martin. "The idea is that those boards in the plant directly link to this one. At one time or another, each of us has brought our entire team up here to look at this board so that they could understand that linkage too. It really helps everyone understand how what they do contributes to what the company is trying to achieve."

"Very good," said Antonio.

As the meeting drew to a close, Yu asked about the inspection report.

"It's due today," said Charlie. Looking at the clock on the wall, he said, "Right now, in fact."

To the whole team he said, "Don't forget we're having

lunch together today. I'll see you all in the canteen in an hour."

Peter appeared at the door. "Just took a call from the Weights guy. There's been some sort of delay. He wouldn't say why, but they're still hoping to get something to us soon."

Charlie looked at Antonio. Both frowned. "I really want certainty on that before going into the directors' meeting this afternoon," said Antonio to Peter. "Uncertainty will start us off on the wrong foot altogether and paint a very negative perception of this plant."

"I'll keep pushing," said Peter.

* * *

"At this point, no matter what happens today, I want to congratulate all of you on your efforts so far," said Charlie to his team as they sat around a large table in the canteen. "I'm confident the 12 per cent savings you've made to date, plus the next 10 per cent that has been identified and mapped out, should be enough for the directors to support us in continuing this project without layoffs. But I don't know what pressure they're under so we'll have to wait and see."

Yu spoke up. "We'd like to thank you, Charlie. Firstly

for surviving your heart attack, so that you could help us through this, and secondly for showing so much faith in us and letting us get on with the job." The group nodded in agreement.

"I'm very glad to have been able to do both of those," said Charlie, smiling. He pointed to the platters on the table and encouraged everyone to eat up. Once again he looked at his watch and wondered what the hold-up could be with the inspectors' report.

As the meal went on Charlie took the time to sit back and observe his leaders. There had been a profound change in them in the last six months. Some had grown enormously: Yu obviously, but even Jerry was far more proactive and supportive of his own team than Charlie would ever have imagined being possible in the past. Martin had a way to go. He was still prone to falling back into 'blame mode' when things went wrong, though recently that had been tempered by the more mature responses he was getting back from others. Most notable in the last month were the far more considered discussions that Jerry and Martin were now having, the results of which had manifested themselves in some outstanding gains in changeover efficiency.

It was only as lunch was wrapping up and the first few

team leaders made to leave that Peter joined them. The look of relief on his face said it all. "The inspection report has just come through … and we're all clear. A couple of minor matters to deal with but overall we passed with flying colors. Great work everyone."

"One down, one to go," said Charlie.

As the day wore on, Charlie sat at his desk trying to work but growing increasingly distracted. The directors' meeting was taking an inordinate amount of time. One after the other his team leaders dropped in hoping for some news but they were all disappointed. As four o'clock approached and there was still no news, Charlie packed his bag and walked to Peter's office.

"I have to go, Peter. Important appointment with my teenage son. He's getting his 'L' plates."

"Shall I put out a state-wide alert?" said Peter. "Sorry, old joke. Go, Charlie. There's nothing you can do here. I'll let you know as soon as I hear something."

⊕ ⊕ ⊕

As Jack sat his traffic laws test, Charlie sat in the waiting room of the roads authority, mobile phone in hand. He checked the screen constantly, but still no message came. Jack's test done – and passed – he dropped his son at home then drove to the doctor's surgery.

"You look a bit distracted," said the doctor a few minutes into Charlie's check-up.

Charlie explained what was happening at the factory.

"Well, let's make this as quick as we can. I don't want to be the cause of aggravating your stress levels," said the doctor.

He ran Charlie through his routine tests then reviewed the last report from the cardiologist.

"You're doing great, Charlie. You've clearly been putting in the effort and now you are starting to see the rewards. The change to your program to include the gym is working. Your weight has fallen off in the last couple of months: down another five kilograms, so that's 10 kilos in six months. Right on target. Blood pressure is good and according to the cardiology report your heart's health is now inside the acceptable limits, if only just. Best of all, there haven't been any scares for a while now."

"The benefits of sticking to the plan," said Charlie.

"Yes indeed," said the doctor.

"So where to from here?" said Charlie.

"I'm happy to stay with the current plan for the next month or two," said the doctor, "after which we'll review again. Once your weight loss reaches 15 kilograms we'll reset things. From then on it will be a case of creating a sustainable lifestyle, rather than a fat-trimming one."

Charlie felt a vibration in his pocket and instinctively put his hand over it.

"Go on, Charlie. Check the message," said the doctor kindly. "I wouldn't normally allow that in my surgery but this is a case of patient health."

Charlie pulled the phone out of his pocket and glanced at the screen. The message said simply, "All good".

The doctor didn't need to be told the news: it was more than clear from Charlie's relieved expression.

"The future's looking good," said the doctor. "For both Charlie and his chocolate factory."

Further information on the concepts explored in this book

The following is a very brief summary of the main concepts addressed in Charlie's story, including pointers to where you can find more information on some of the major topics. While the story revolves around a chocolate factory, these concepts have much broader applicability, not only to other manufacturing situations but also to service businesses (banking, insurance, etc.), hospitality, health care – any organization really.

People Skills

Early in the book Charlie is reminded of the importance of *delegation* and the role that delegating responsibility and accountability can play in both sharing the load and *empowering* employees. Empowerment increases ownership and encourages creativity: something both Charlie's team leaders and their staff learnt from their experiences.

Another lesson learnt by everyone involved was the power of *collaboration*: how working together on a common goal, openly sharing knowledge and ultimately relying on each other all led to better results for everyone.

A point returned to throughout this book is the importance of keeping the *customer at the center* of your decision making. Constantly asking "Would my customers be happy that I am doing this?" or "Would my customers be happy to be paying for this?" puts a fresh perspective on wasted time, wasted movement and so on.

Of course, effectively asking questions like these requires *learning to see* what is really going on. Charlie and his people learned about the Japanese concept of going to *gemba* − going to where the action is and watching, carefully, what is actually going on. For managers, this means moving away from the desk and spending time where the work is happening: in the office, in the field, or on the factory floor. For operators and line managers, it means taking the time to stand back and really look at what is happening, questioning everything − especially preconceived ideas − asking "Why do we do that?" over and over, and treating the underlying root causes of problems rather than the immediately presenting symptoms. Assume nothing and be willing to try anything.

Having recognized waste in all its forms, there next needs to be a *willingness to change*. As Charlie learnt, but also as his factory learnt, often we resist change until an accident, disaster or some form of immediate threat forces us to act. In a lean environment, there is a much more open and constant willingness to change. There is a culture of trying things out to see if they will work, of making change not because it is essential but because it will improve things for the customer (and in turn for the organization).

Promoting all these things – empowerment, collaboration, customer centricity, learning to see, willingness to change, and so on – is what *lean leadership* is all about. (For further information on the concepts behind what I call *lean leadership*, I recommend the book *Toyota Kata* by Mike Rother.)

Best Practice Methodologies

The PDCA Board described in this book is a version of a board more widely known as a 'strategy deployment' board or a 'Hoshin' board. *Hoshin Kanri* is a Japanese term describing a method for developing, sharing and tracking corporate goals in a way that links actions at all levels of the organization back to those goals. This book describes just one way of designing and implementing a Hoshin board. It is a simplified example – designed to give the reader a practical approach to achieving results when a mandated goal has been set – in that the Hoshin goal set in the story starts with the target of 20 per cent cost reductions. A more complete Hoshin Kanri implementation would start a step 'above' this, developing a business strategy from which a 20 per cent cut in costs might result. It is important to note also that, as described in the book, a goal like a 20 per cent cost reduction would rarely require an equal contribution from each department, as this would most likely be counterproductive.

The *PDCA cycle* described in this book (Plan – Do – Check – Adjust) is a variation on a very similar cycle widely used in manufacturing, engineering and elsewhere. That PDCA cycle simply uses the term 'act' where we have used 'adjust'. Often the PDCA cycle is seen as something to be used for specific projects (there is a parallel here with the DMAIC cycle used in the Six Sigma methodology), whereas in practice, as we saw in Chapter 6, PDCA can be applied every day to quite small situations.

More information on Hoshin Kanri and PDCA can be found in the following books:

- *Hoshin Handbook*, Third Edition, by Pete Babich (published by Total Quality Engineering Inc., 2006)
- *Getting the Right Things Done: A leader's guide to planning and execution* by Pascal Dennis (published by Lean Enterprise Institute, 2006).

In Chapter 5 Charlie introduces the concept of *visual management* to his team. Visual management is widely used by Japanese manufacturers and many Western manufacturers as a way of conveying production status information in a current, easy-to-read format. Its principles, and adaptations of many of the visual management tools described here, are widely applicable. Visual management is an important tool in the sustaining of delegation and shared accountability, as it makes public situations that might otherwise be buried in management reports. While visual management tools can be quite complex (as with the Andon lights described in the story, or the Hoshin board), they can also be very simple (e.g. the streamers used on fans in Chapter 6). The main intention of any tool should be to make any abnormality easy to spot at a glance.

The table below summarizes some of the main concepts covered in this book and draws parallels with the health challenges faced by Charlie. You can find a surprising number of parallels between personal challenges and business challenges – and the ways to meet those challenges – when you look for them.

Improving business	Improving health
Warning signs of a business health problem include: - low morale - blaming - unwillingness to be flexible - lack of ownership	**Warning signs** of a personal health problem include include: - low self esteem - low energy - unwillingness to be flexible - lack of willpower
Fundamentally change the way you run your business	**Fundamentally change** the way you run your life
Trim waste to improve productivity	**Trim fat** to improve health
Sustainable change is the only way to succeed	**Sustainable change** is the only way to succeed
Plan 20% cut in costs **Do** reduce waste and inefficiency **Check** that changes are working **Adjust** to increase benefits	**Plan** 20% cut in weight **Do** improve diet and increase exercise **Check** that changes are working **Adjust** to accelerate gains
Measure the results (cost reductions), not the effort (hours worked)	**Measure the results** (weight loss) not the effort (number of visits to gym)

Collection Website

Downloadable tools you can use in your own work are available by registering at *www.aleanbook.com*. Enter the promotional code L2E0A1D2 when prompted after registration for access to additional, reader-only materials.

About the author

Marta Ferreira Böing is a passionate advocate for the application of lean principles and methodologies to operations management, and the benefits this can bring to both organizations and their employees. She has worked in this area for her entire career, as a manager, consultant and educator.

Marta initially studied mechanical engineering and a Master of Science in Operations Management in Europe before moving to Australia. There she joined automotive supplier TriMas Corporation where she was promoted to Production Manager in just three months. In her next role at Yazaki Corporation (Australian Arrow) she earned the opportunity to travel to Japan and observe lean principles and practices as applied by the pioneers of process improvement.

In 2007, Marta joined the ANZ Bank as Lean Advisor to the Managing Director, Operations. Since then she has driven the ongoing translation and implementation of lean principles into the banking environment. She has developed extensive and widely used training and leadership development programs, and taken a hands-on role with a number of cultural change initiatives. As Head of Global Operational Excellence, Marta manages a team that supports behavior change programs for the bank across all divisions and regions (in 48 countries), promoting a lean and continuous improvement culture.

Both staff and senior management at the ANZ have recognized Marta's work by selecting her to receive a number of prominent awards. She is also recognized for her expertise, having been invited to speak at the conferences of a diverse range of industry groups including health care, government, manufacturing and tertiary education.

This is Marta's second book and the first in her new series of books aimed at supporting the application of lean principles. Each book will demonstrate a different aspect of 'lean thinking' applied to a different industry sector.

1 – Challenge